AI and Third-Party Risk

Solutions for Assessing and Managing Your AI Vendors and Systems

Gregory C. Rasner
Maria C. Rasner

Apress®

AI and Third-Party Risk: Solutions for Assessing and Managing Your AI Vendors and Systems

Gregory C. Rasner
Washington, DC, USA

Maria C. Rasner
Washington, DC, USA

ISBN-13 (pbk): 979-8-8688-2464-7
ISBN-13 (electronic): 979-8-8688-2465-4
https://doi.org/10.1007/979-8-8688-2465-4

Managing Director, Apress Media LLC: Welmoed Spahr
Acquisitions Editor: Susan McDermott
Project Manager: Jessica Vakili

Distributed to the book trade worldwide by Springer Science+Business Media New York, 1 New York Plaza, New York, NY 10004. Phone 1-800-SPRINGER, fax (201) 348-4505, e-mail orders-ny@springer-sbm.com, or visit www.springeronline.com. Apress Media, LLC is a Delaware LLC and the sole member (owner) is Springer Science + Business Media Finance Inc (SSBM Finance Inc). SSBM Finance Inc is a **Delaware** corporation.

For information on translations, please e-mail booktranslations@springernature.com; for reprint, paperback, or audio rights, please e-mail bookpermissions@springernature.com.

Apress titles may be purchased in bulk for academic, corporate, or promotional use. eBook versions and licenses are also available for most titles. For more information, reference our Print and eBook Bulk Sales web page at http://www.apress.com/bulk-sales.

If disposing of this product, please recycle the paper

We dedicate this book first to God and then to our kids (Christian, Gregory Jr., and Kristina) and our grandkids (Ilauna and Eli). We are blessed to be able to write this book and share our knowledge with others.

Table of Contents

About the Authors

Gregory Rasner (CISSP, CIPM, ITIL, CCNA) is the founder and CEO of Third Party Threat Hunting LLC, bringing his extensive expertise in third-party, supply chain, and cybersecurity risk to the market. He authored the books *Cybersecurity & Third-Party Risk: Third Party Threat Hunting* (Wiley, 2021), *Zero Trust and Third-Party Risk* (Wiley, 2023), and *Privileged Access Management: Strategies for Zero Trust in the Enterprise* (Apress, 2025) and developed the internationally recognized training and certification program “Third-Party Cyber Risk Assessor” (TPCRA) (Third Party Risk Association, 2023) and other training programs. He is a regular keynote speaker and panelist on cybersecurity and risk management topics, also contributing to blogs, podcasts, and online articles. Greg has held leadership roles across the finance, healthcare, biotech, high-tech, and manufacturing sectors and earned his BA from Claremont McKenna College.

Maria Rasner (CISM, CCZK, CCSK, TAISE) has years of extensive Identity and Access Management and Privileged Access Management experience. Maria is the co-author of the book *Privileged Access Management: Strategies for Zero Trust in the Enterprise* (Apress, 2025). She has run the governance, remediation, and implementation of small and large IAM and PAM programs, both on-premises and in the cloud. Her experience and certifications include cloud IAM and PAM experience in AWS and Azure cloud environments. Maria has several articles to her credit on the topic of Cloud PAM Security published in the ISSA Online Journal and IDSA website. Maria has strong enthusiasm for continuous learning, always exploring new developments in AI. She has taken the Google AI Essentials training as well as Stanford University's Deep Learning Specialization course. Maria is a member of Cloud Security Alliance's AI Controls Framework Working Group responsible for the publication of AI Controls Matrix (AICM). She's also certified in TAISE (Trusted AI Safety Expert).

About the Technical Reviewer

Julie Gaiaschi CISA, CISM, is the CEO and Co-Founder of the Third Party Risk Association (TPRA). She has over 15 years of technology and information security risk experience, with the last ten years specializing in third-party risk identification and mitigation techniques. In her role as CEO, she provides strategic direction for the non-profit, whose mission it is to further the third-party risk profession through knowledge sharing and networking. She also has a passion for helping others enhance their own third-party risk management programs. In 2021, Julie was awarded CEO of the Year by Women in Governance, Risk, and Compliance.

Prior to co-founding the TPRA, Julie consulted on third-party risk for a large bank. She also developed and led a large health payer organization's Third Party Security program. There, she established and executed the third-party risk assessment process, which included integration into the procurement process. Prior to her role as the leader over Third Party Security, Julie was a Senior IT Auditor.

Julie resides in Iowa with her husband and two girls. She enjoys traveling and cooking.

CHAPTER 1

Artificial Intelligence and Third-Party Risk

Disruptive Times

> *"Artificial intelligence is going to replace literally half of all white-collar workers in the U.S.," Ford Motor Chief Executive Jim Farley said this summer (2025).*[1]

As we reach the middle of the 2020s and look ahead, it is exciting to see how much of the future has already become part of our present. Artificial Intelligence (AI) is transforming our daily lives in incredible ways. What once belonged to the realm of science fiction is now a vibrant part of reality, with AI making a difference in activities, from helping with homework and archaeology to advancing pharmaceutical research and software development. Although the reasons for and methods of AI's application can differ widely, one thing is clear: its presence is strong and growing every day.

[1] https://www.wsj.com/tech/ai/walmart-ceo-doug-mcmillon-ai-job-losses-dbaca3aa?mod=hp_lead_pos1

G. C. Rasner, M. C. Rasner, *AI and Third-Party Risk*,
https://doi.org/10.1007/979-8-8688-2465-4_1

In disruptive terms, there are already effects on employment. Artificial Intelligence is causing a loss of roles, usually entry-level, in a few key sectors that are mostly using this new capability. Software developers aged 22 to 25 have experienced a 20% decrease in headcount since 2022. There are fewer jobs available today for technology workers in late 2025 than there were previously, especially for those without AI skills.[2] Walmart's CEO, Doug McMillon, in September 2025, stated that "AI Is going to change literally every job."[3] In fact, the biggest employer in the United States, Walmart, is going to expand stores and services over the next three years, but headcount is expected to stay flat "as AI eliminates or transforms roles."[4]

The demand for workers with AI skills is on the opposite end of the spectrum in terms of demand and supply. The job market for entry-level workers outside this field continues to decline while AI roles are on the rise. In addition, those with zero to three years of AI experience are seeing salaries increase by 12% in just one year. Many entry-level candidates are in their 20s and receiving offers worth millions a year. It is skewing the labor market for workers who just a few years ago were themselves in high demand in favor of fields many only heard of in the movies or books.[5]

Times haven't been this disruptive because of technology since the late 1990s and early 2000s, during the dot-com era that highlighted the Internet's influence on the global economy and society. This current

---

[2] https://www.wsj.com/articles/it-unemployment-fell-in-august-but-the-tech-jobs-market-is-still-shrinking-e80225e3?mod=Searchresults&pos=1&page=1

[3] https://www.wsj.com/tech/ai/walmart-ceo-doug-mcmillon-ai-job-losses-dbaca3aa?mod=hp_lead_pos1

[4] https://www.wsj.com/tech/ai/walmart-ceo-doug-mcmillon-ai-job-losses-dbaca3aa?mod=hp_lead_pos1

[5] https://www.wsj.com/tech/ai/ai-jobs-entry-level-salary-ab2a11c0?mod=Searchresults&pos=6&page=1

change is impactful, with faster and more dramatic shifts than ever before. Throughout history, there have been other significant technological revolutions, like the printing press, railroads, telegraphs, automobiles, and personal computers.

As the teams managing third-party and supply chain risk at organizations already struggle with rapid changes in regulatory guidance, the introduction of Artificial Intelligence comes along to both complicate and improve matters. It complicates matters because it adds to an already complex world and set of risks. It can also make things better in several ways, which we will explore in this book, such as reducing resource requirements and enhancing risk detection and accuracy.

Ultimately, AI is just another risk we need to recognize, understand, and manage. Although it can be quite complex and not fully understood by many, it remains simply a risk to handle. The goal of this book is to make AI safer and easier to understand, so you can more confidently identify, assess, and manage AI risks within your organization and your third-party ecosystem. Keep in mind, AI systems often work with sensitive information and can make decisions independently. Their complexity, lack of transparency, and reliance on external components can introduce new vulnerabilities that typical security measures might overlook.

Primers and Preparation

This publication is intended for all business professionals, regardless of their specific occupation or background, to help understand AI concepts and support their practical use in workplaces and organizations. Because the audience has different levels of experience and focus, some sections will summarize the key ideas that will form the basis for the next chapters. This will make sure that no reader misses important information. For experienced professionals in AI, cybersecurity, risk, third-party risk, or risk management frameworks, it might seem okay to skip these sections. However, it is best to review them to ensure no important details are missed in this short but important part. Readers are strongly encouraged to carefully review these sections to make sure the logic and ideas match what is expected and what follows.

Artificial Intelligence and History[6]

AI is a term that few used a couple of years ago, but now it is being integrated into everything today. It can be defined as the creation of a system capable of performing tasks that usually require human intelligence, such as learning, problem-solving, reasoning, and decision-making. Artificial Intelligence can encompass a wide range of technologies, from machine learning to deep learning.

The history of Artificial Intelligence dates back hundreds of years, but the key milestone arrived in 1950 when Alan Turing first coined the term "AI" and introduced the idea of a thinking machine that could potentially outperform a human. A benchmark was developed to evaluate an AI system's behavior against that of humans, called the Turing Test.

In 1956, a summer workshop at Dartmouth College involved some key early leaders in this field, where "Artificial Intelligence" was first officially established as a field of study. In the 1960s and 1970s, some early research and funding were available for AI development, but relatively little work was conducted during this period.

In the 1980s, there was a resurgence of neural networks trained by algorithms. In 1997, a milestone was reached when IBM's Deep Blue defeated the then-world chess champion Garry Kasparov, astonishing many with the advancements of thinking machines. The early 2000s saw significant progress in computer processing power, large datasets, and algorithm improvements that laid the groundwork for later success.

[6] https://www.ibm.com/think/topics/history-of-artificial-intelligence#:~:text=1952,Shannon%20from%20Bell%20Telephone%20Laboratories.

The 2010s saw an increase in effort and success in AI. IBM's Watson defeated human champions on the game show "Jeopardy!" in 2011, and the growing power of graphic processing units (GPUs) provided a springboard into the 2020s and the availability of generative AI models like ChatGPT, which have led to the current "AI boom."

Primer

The Oxford English Dictionary defines AI as "The capacity of computers or other machines to exhibit or simulate intelligent behavior; the field of study concerned with this." There are three components to AI.

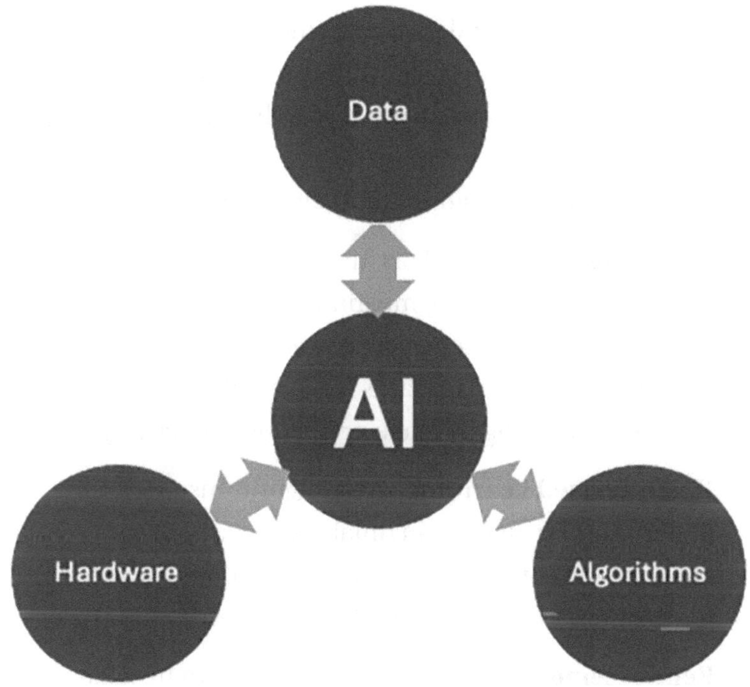

Figure 1-1. *Three Parts of AI*

Algorithms

Algorithms are step-by-step instructions or procedures that a computer follows to solve a specific problem or perform a particular task. These algorithms have been around for a long time, such as "Linear Regression" and others. It is essentially linear algebra. AI algorithms are sets of instructions that enable machines to learn from data, identify patterns, and make decisions to perform tasks like speech recognition and problem-solving.

One key concept about AI algorithms is that they detect patterns and relationships in data. This process is called training. AI algorithms rely on data. The quality and quantity of data are essential for an algorithm's effectiveness; more and better data lead to more accurate predictions and decisions. Ultimately, the best AI algorithms to use depend on the specific task or problem they aim to solve, with researchers choosing and training models accordingly.

There are three major categories of AI algorithms.

- **Supervised Learning**: This involves algorithms that learn from labeled data, meaning the input data already includes the correct answers. These methods are especially useful for tasks like classification and regression, helping us make predictions effectively.
- **Unsupervised Learning**: These algorithms discover patterns and structures in unlabeled data without knowing the correct answers ahead of time. They're used for tasks such as anomaly detection.
- **Reinforcement Learning**: Algorithms learn by taking actions and getting feedback, whether that's a reward or a penalty, in a specific environment. This approach of trial and error helps them figure out the best strategies.

Algorithms work in four steps:

1. **Data Input**: Algorithms need huge amounts of data as input to be able to make decisions or predictions.
2. **Model Training**: Algorithms use mathematical methods to adjust internal parameters, helping identify patterns and relationships in the data.
3. **Prediction/Decision**: Once trained, the algorithm can predict, classify new data, or make decisions on unseen inputs.
4. **Feedback and Growth**: Algorithms have the ability to learn from their mistakes. By using feedback loops, they can continually improve and become more accurate over time, making them better at what they do.

Hardware

This essential element depended on having enough computing power to run the algorithms and handle the data effectively. It's only recently that GPU technology has advanced enough to process the complex calculations and large datasets needed to generate meaningful results. Nowadays, cloud services and high-powered computing accelerators make it possible for AI to operate on a much larger scale, opening up exciting new possibilities.

AI hardware comprises both versatile components like CPUs and specialized ones such as GPUs, TPUs, NPUs, and FPGAs. These components are specifically designed to handle the demanding computations required for AI and machine learning. They offer the vital processing power and unique architectures necessary for training AI models on big datasets, supporting a wide range of applications from detailed image analysis to large language processing.

There are a few types of AI hardware to be aware of at this time:

- **Central Processing Units**: The main component of a computer that can handle most computational tasks, but isn't usually the best fit for the heavy computing needs of AI training.
- **Graphics Processing Units (GPUs)**: Extremely efficient for parallel processing, GPUs are a leading platform for training AI models because they speed up tasks like neural network training.
- **Tensor Processing Units (TPUs)**: Designed specifically for AI and machine learning, TPUs are custom-built by companies like Google. They focus on high-throughput, low-precision calculations to speed up certain AI workloads.
- **Application-Specific Integrated Circuits (ASICs)**: Custom-built hardware designed to boost specific AI tasks, delivering unmatched efficiency for particular workloads.
- **Neural Processing Units (NPUs)**: General-purpose integrated circuits built to work alongside CPUs and GPUs, speeding up AI tasks in consumer devices.
- **Field-Programmable Gate Arrays (FPGAs)**: Reconfigurable integrated circuits that provide flexibility and cost-efficiency for various AI applications.
- **Wafer-Scale Engines**: A type of processor known for providing massive computational power with numerous AI compute cores.

Hardware plays several roles in AI. First, it provides computational power. AI hardware supplies the massive processing capability needed to handle large datasets and run complex algorithms. It enables efficient storage and management of data necessary for training and deploying AI models. Specialized hardware components, such as tensor cores, are designed with architectures optimized for the specific calculations AI requires. Energy efficiency has become a growing concern, not only because of climate impact but also because future power demands may exceed planned electrical loads. Often, AI-specific hardware is designed to be more energy-efficient than general-purpose components, which is crucial for large-scale AI deployments.

Data

Most people recognize this key element because, without data, AI cannot exist. Currently, the world stores and manages Zettabytes: trillions of gigabytes of data. This data is critical for AI systems to learn and predict outcomes. Data acts as the raw material that powers and trains AI, helping it identify patterns, make predictions, and execute tasks by providing essential information for processing and understanding. Without sufficient quality and quantity of data whether structured or unstructured, collected from diverse sources, and properly labeled or annotated, AI models cannot develop the skills and intelligence needed to function, improve, or generate valuable insights.

AI leverages data in multiple ways. For one, it's used to train models. By analyzing vast amounts of data, AI algorithms can recognize patterns and learn relationships, making them more sophisticated and accurate. The more data an AI system processes, the better it becomes at handling complex tasks. AI also uses data to make predictions and informed decisions by analyzing historical data and identifying trends. Additionally, AI techniques can quickly and accurately analyze large datasets, revealing hidden patterns, trends, and insights that might be overlooked by human analysts. Data is essential for various AI applications, including facial recognition, natural language processing, and time-series analysis.

There are important factors to consider regarding the quality, quantity, and structure of data in AI. When focusing on quality, it is essential that the data be clean, accurate, and relevant to ensure AI models function properly and produce reliable results. This involves steps like data cleaning, validation, and labeling. Additionally, a large volume of data is necessary for AI models to learn effectively and become more capable; after all, more data helps in better pattern recognition. Data can also be either structured, such as in databases, or unstructured, like text, images, or audio. While AI systems are designed to handle both types, some preparation might be required to get everything ready.

AI Development Life Cycle

We now have a new acronym to memorize: AI-DLC, which stands for Artificial Intelligence Development Life Cycle. AI refers to software, and there is a well-known acronym for that area: SDLC, for Software or Secure Development Life Cycle. One can follow their existing SDLC when developing AI products and services; however, there are some differences and risks unique to AI, making adopting the AI-DLC a wise choice.

Creating and deploying artificial intelligence systems involves several essential stages. The process starts with defining the problem and collecting data. Next, the data is prepared and features are engineered.[7] Then, a model is chosen and its architecture is designed. This is followed by a training phase, where algorithms learn from the prepared data. To ensure the model performs well, it is validated and tested. The model is

[7] "Generative AI Security: Theories and Practices," by Ken Huang et al., Springer, 2024, pp.259–266.

further refined through iterations based on the results. Once ready, the AI system is deployed into production environments. After deployment, its performance is monitored, any drift is addressed, and the model is updated as needed.

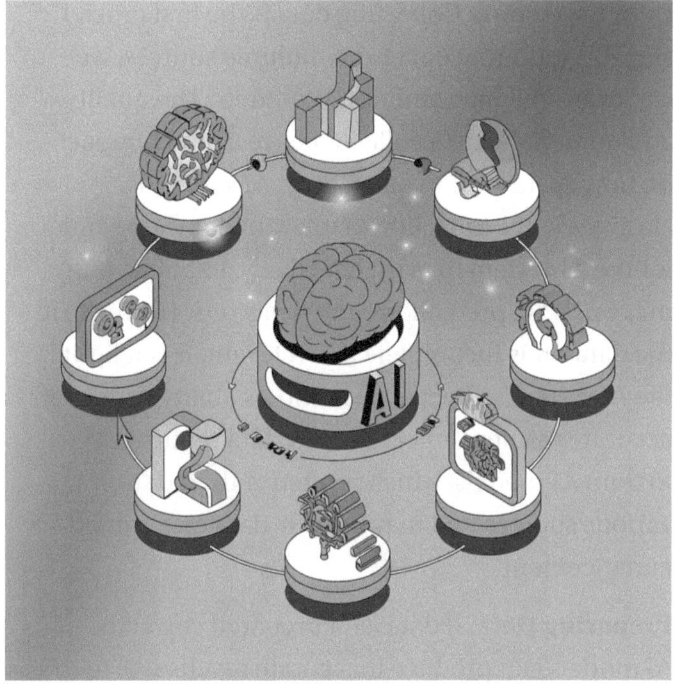

Figure 1-2. *AI Development Life Cycle*

There are eight phases for the AI development life cycle:

1. **Defining the Problem**: The AI development life cycle starts with defining the problem, where we determine the objectives and requirements of the AI solution. This crucial first step lays the groundwork for the entire AI project. Clearly define the problem boundaries, outlining what's included and excluded from the project scope. Identify and involve all relevant stakeholders,

from end users to executives, to understand their viewpoints and needs. Gather and document both functional and non-functional requirements through interviews, workshops, and surveys.

2. **Data Collection**: Collecting data is the first crucial step. By gathering data from multiple sources, we can train, validate, and test AI models. The quality and quantity of data collected have a direct impact on how accurate and efficient an AI system is. Having a solid collection of relevant data is essential for the AI system to learn effectively, enabling it to make precise predictions and decisions. However, if the data set is incomplete or irrelevant, it can limit the AI system's effectiveness and its ability to deliver accurate results. Collect the raw data required to train AI models, which is often gathered from various sources and may include data creation or enhancement.

3. **Preparing Data**: If data isn't prepared correctly, AI models can produce inaccurate results due to poor quality or inconsistent data. By refining the data, the AI system is better equipped to learn, predict, and make decisions, ensuring more accurate and reliable results. To do this, identify missing values, outliers, and inconsistencies in the dataset using suitable techniques, and remove or correct inaccuracies, duplicates, and irrelevant data. Normalize or scale the data to improve model performance, which may include encoding categorical variables or breaking down complex

variables. Also, implement efficient and accurate data labeling processes, using crowdsourcing or semi-supervised learning methods when possible.

4. **Model Design**: During the model design phase of the AI development life cycle, AI engineers choose the most suitable algorithms and techniques based on the problem at hand and the available data. The selected model type can influence the performance of an AI system whether it involves supervised learning, unsupervised learning, reinforcement learning models, or others. This phase involves defining the model's architecture, such as the number of layers and nodes in a neural network. The success of this stage sets the foundation for effective training, validation, and testing, ultimately resulting in more reliable and accurate outcomes.

5. **Model Training**: After designing the model, the next step is training it. This involves exposing the model to the prepared data, which it uses to learn patterns and relationships. As a result, the model improves its ability to make predictions or decisions based on data. The training process continues until the model reaches a satisfactory level of accuracy. Algorithms are crucial in this process, adjusting the model's internal parameters to minimize errors. It's essential to note that the quality of training directly impacts the effectiveness of the AI system, as well-trained models lead to accurate and reliable predictions.

6. **Model Evaluation**: Once the training phase is complete, the AI model's performance must be evaluated using a separate validation dataset. This new dataset is used to test the model's ability to produce accurate results, as it's never been seen before. To assess the model's effectiveness, metrics such as precision, recall, accuracy, and F1 score are used. If the model's performance falls short, it's sent back for further training or adjustment. Building a robust and reliable AI system that can deliver accurate results in real-world scenarios relies on this iterative process.

7. **Model Deployment**: After successfully training and evaluating the model, it is deployed into the production environment, where it can start working with new data. It will make predictions and deliver results either in real time or in batches, depending on what the project needs. You can choose to deploy it on the cloud, on-premises, or at the edge, based on your specific requirements. Using containerization tools helps keep deployment consistent across different environments. Don't forget to include load balancing and scaling strategies to help the model perform well, even when the load varies. This approach makes the deployment process smoother and more reliable.

8. **Model Monitoring**: Once the AI model is deployed, monitoring is key to ensure it performs optimally over time. By regularly checking the model's performance against its predictions

using relevant metrics and feedback, any drop in accuracy or effectiveness serves as a signal to refine or retrain the model, closing the life cycle loop. This continuous process is crucial for the AI's adaptability and long-term success in dynamic real-world applications.

Every phase of the AI development life cycle is connected, so it needs smooth transitions and ongoing feedback to make sure the system works as intended and meets the highest standards for AI security and efficiency.

Types of AI Models[8]

AI can be categorized by a couple of buckets: by capability (Narrow, General, and Super AI); by function (Reactive, Limited Memory, Theory of Mind, and Self-Aware); and by technology (Machine Learning, Deep Learning, Natural Language Processing). By capability, we can expand on definitions:

Artificial Narrow Intelligence (ANI) or Weak AI: This AI is created for a specific task or a limited set of tasks. Examples include voice assistants like Siri or Alexa, self-driving cars, and recommendation engines.

Artificial General Intelligence (AGI) or Strong AI: At the time of this writing, it is still hypothetical and would be a human-level intelligence that can understand, learn, and apply learned knowledge to any task a human can do.

Artificial Superintelligence (ASI) is similar to AGI, but it's still just a concept at this point. It's envisioned as an AI that surpasses human intelligence and abilities in every way. While it's currently theoretical,

[8] "Generative AI Security: Theories and Practices," by Ken Huang et al., Springer, 2024, pp.6–11.

many believe it's only a matter of time and increased processing power before we see it become a reality.

Figure 1-3. *Artificial Superintelligence*

By function, there are four classifications of AI:

Reactive Machines are the most basic of AI types, and these typically react to situations, but cannot form memories or use past experiences to make new decisions. The example most often used here is a chess-playing machine.

Limited Memory AI can store past experiences or data for a short period to inform future decisions. Self-driving cars are a great example of this, as they use limited memory to help navigate traffic patterns and roads.

Theory of Mind AI is a more advanced type of AI that includes an understanding of human emotions, intentions, and beliefs. Self-Aware AI is the most advanced form of AI that possesses consciousness and is self-aware. Both of these last two types are theoretical.

The types of technology AI are:

Machine Learning is a key branch of AI that enables systems to learn from data without needing to be programmed explicitly each time. Machine learning models can analyze data, recognize patterns, predict outcomes, and enhance system accuracy over time. Machine Learning will continue to evolve and learn from experience. Unlike traditional AI, which operates on fixed rules, Machine Learning will continually evolve with experience and feedback. As you can see from Figure 1-4, Deep Learning (DL) is a subset of Machine Learning (ML) that is very specialized. This is designed to mimic the structure of the human brain with the use of neural networks. The neural networks created enable the machine to recognize complex and hard-to-see objects due to large data sets. The DL systems can also make sophisticated decisions.

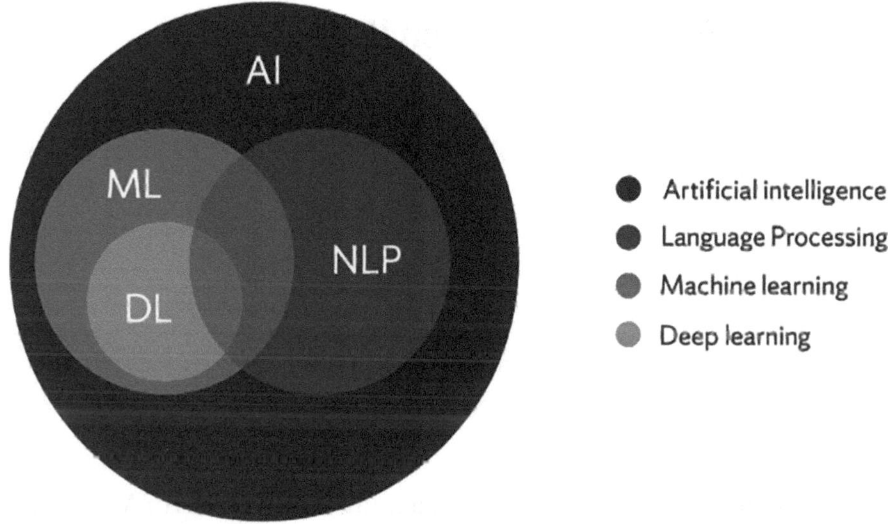

Figure 1-4. *AI Types*[9]

[9] https://ischool.syracuse.edu/types-of-ai/

Natural language processing (NLP) is also a subset of AI that is very reliant on ML and DL for recognizing patterns, understanding human language, and allowing for predictive output. NLP enables the machine to understand, interpret, and respond to normal human language. This requires the combination of machine learning and deep learning to process text and speech.

There are some key aspects of Artificial Intelligence. First is cognitive functions, where AI will replicate functions typical of the human mind, such as perception, reasoning, and interaction with the environment. AI should be able to learn from data and improve its performance over time without significant human oversight. AI systems are designed to perform complex tasks that range from analyzing terabytes of data and then making predictions about probable next outcomes to automating repetitive tasks.

Table of AI Types and Common Uses

Type of AI Model	Supervised Learning	Unsupervised Learning	Reinforcement Learning
Common Use	Diagnosis, Predictive Analysis, Spam and fraud detection	Anomaly Detection, mage & Speech Clustering, Association	Processing Natural Language Processing (NLP) Autonomous Systems
Use Case	Facial recognition Email Filtering	Fraud detection Market analysis	Drones, Self-driving cars Chatbots

Prompts

Most AIs require some prompting from a human or system. An AI prompt is the input, instruction, question, or command that the user provides to an artificial intelligence model to guide it in generating the output requested. Effective prompts are clear, specific, and provide sufficient context for the AI to understand the user's intent and produce an appropriate and high-quality result.

These prompts break down into two main categories: task-based and technique-based. Task-based prompts are designed to specify a particular task for the AI to perform. Types of task-based prompts are

- **Text Generation Prompts**: Ask the AI to create written content, such as articles, stories, or poems.
- **Summarization Prompts**: Guide the AI to produce concise summaries of longer texts.
- **Translation Prompts**: Instruct the AI to convert text from one language to another.
- **Question Answering Prompts**: Elicit direct answers to questions based on the AI's training data.
- **Code Generation Prompts**: Request the AI to write code snippets or programs.
- **Image Generation Prompts**: Direct the AI to create visual artwork, illustrations, or designs.
- **Classification Prompts**: Ask the AI to categorize or label information, such as classifying a review as positive or negative.
- **Dialogue Generation Prompts**: Prompt the AI to engage in conversational interactions and simulate dialogue.

There are four types of Technique-based prompts:

- **Zero-Shot Prompting**: Have the model complete a task without any previous examples of it.
- **Few-Shot Prompting**: Give the AI a few examples of the task it's supposed to do before asking it to complete the task itself.

- **Chain-of-Thought (CoT) Prompting**: Help the AI break down a problem into smaller steps, making its answer more logical.
- **Contextual Prompts**: Provide the AI with background info or specific context to help it give more relevant and accurate answers.

There are a few other prompt types that don't fall into these two neat categories:

- **Creative Prompts**: Aim to generate distinctive and imaginative content, including stylized writing or original ideas.
- **Instructional Prompts**: Provide guidance on procedures, steps, or specific instructions to the AI.
- **Informational Prompts**: Similar to a search engine, these prompts collect and synthesize information from the AI's knowledge base or uploaded resources.
- **Listicle Prompts**: Request the AI to compile lists of items, ideas, or themes.

Agents

Another key area in AI is agents. An AI agent is a software system that uses artificial intelligence to carry out tasks, make decisions, and adapt to meet specific goals on a user's behalf. Unlike basic chatbots, AI agents can operate independently, using reasoning, planning, and memory to process information, utilize tools, and take action in their environment without constant human oversight. These agents draw on techniques like large language models (LLMs), natural language processing (NLP), and machine learning to interact with external systems and learn over time, making them valuable tools for complex workflows and automation across various fields. AI agents work with five steps:

1. **Goal Setting**: A human user establishes the overarching objective for the AI agent.

2. **Perception and Processing**: The agent gathers pertinent data from its environment.

3. **Reasoning and Planning**: The agent utilizes its AI capabilities to determine the necessary steps and appropriate tools.

4. **Action and Execution**: The agent executes the selected actions, frequently involving a multi-step, iterative process.

5. **Learning and Adaptation**: The agent assesses the outcomes of its actions and refines its approach for future tasks, thereby learning from experience.

There are some key characteristics of an AI agent:

- **Goal-oriented**: AI agents are built with specific objectives and work to accomplish them.

- **Autonomy**: They can make decisions and take actions on their own, without needing step-by-step instructions from a human.

- **Perception**: AI agents collect information from their environment through various inputs, such as text, voice, or data from APIs and other tools.

- **Reasoning and Planning**: They analyze the data they gather to choose the best way to reach their goal.

- **Action**: After reasoning, agents perform actions, which may include generating outputs, communicating with users, or interacting with software and external systems.
- **Memory and Learning**: AI agents can remember information across tasks and over time, improving their performance and adjusting to user expectations.
- **Tools**: They commonly use different external tools and systems (like web browsers, code interpreters, or APIs) to gather more information or complete complex tasks.

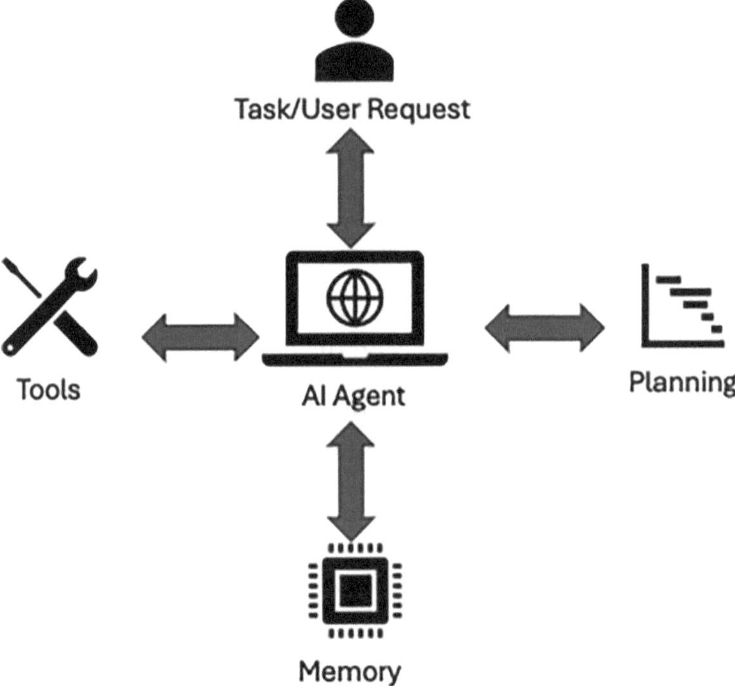

Figure 1-5. *AI Agent's Inputs*

There are many examples of AI agents in our lives currently, such as in customer service settings, where an agent can resolve customer queries by accessing internal documentation and providing solutions. In software development, an agent can analyze problems, generate code, and optimize processes. In the marketing space, an AI agent can automate and optimize global marketing campaigns, delivering results faster than a human.

Artificial intelligence is a new tool and technology that our business partners and vendors are going to use. As we said at the beginning of this section, AI is a risk. It isn't magic; it is math and data done at scale. As we've described what AI is, what it contains, and the types and parts of it in this section, this knowledge will build into how we identify, assess, and manage the AI risk presented by our vendors and partners.

AI Risks in Real Life

It always helps to illustrate the risk of an item by demonstrating how bad it can get. Examples of AI-related data breaches highlight some concerning incidents. For instance, the Clearview AI case involved personal images being scraped without consent, and the TaskRabbit incident saw AI-driven DDoS attacks that exposed customer data. Breaches can also happen through maliciously created content, such as AI-generated phishing emails. Additionally, breaches may occur when employees misuse AI chatbots by inputting sensitive information, as reported in Dutch DPA notifications where a GP entered medical records and a telecom company shared customer data. These incidents remind us of the importance of safeguarding our data and staying vigilant. Since AI use is new, there aren't years and years of data, but there are four significant examples:

- **TaskRabbit**: Here, hackers leveraged AI-powered bots to launch a sophisticated Distributed Denial of Service (DDoS) attack, ultimately leading to customer data theft (2025).

- **Dutch DPA Notifications**: According to the Netherlands' data protection authority, there have been cases where employees misused AI chatbots by entering sensitive patient medical data and customer addresses, violating company agreements (2024).
- **Yum! Brand**: The company faced an AI-driven ransomware attack that affected both employee and corporate data, resulting in the shutdown of many UK operations branches (2023).
- **Clearview AI**: A Facial recognition company came under fire for gathering billions of images from social media to train its AI model, sparking concerns about privacy and consent (2020).

There are also some examples of the common risks for AI in real life to demonstrate that this is already occurring.

- **AI Bias**: A study done by researchers at MIT's Computer Science and AI Lab found that risk prediction algorithms were shown to have a racial bias.[10]
- **AI Bias**: Studies by Carnegie Mellon University found that online ads offering help in finding jobs paying over $200,000 were shown to significantly fewer women than men, sparking concerns about the fairness of online ad targeting.[11]

[10] https://news.mit.edu/2022/when-subtle-biases-ai-influence-emergency-decisions-1216

[11] https://www.cmu.edu/news/stories/archives/2015/july/online-ads-research.html#:~:text=Experiments%20by%20Carnegie%20Mellon%20University,fairness%20of%20targeting%20ads%20online.

- **AI Hallucinations**: Air Canada's AI-powered chatbot kindly offered a passenger a bereavement discount, mentioning that if they used it within the next 90 days, a part of their ticket costs would be refunded. When the passenger tried to claim this, Air Canada explained that they don't offer refunds for trips that have already happened. This is just a matter of policy.[12]
- **AI Lack of Transparency**: In 2014, Amazon created an AI tool to automate resume screening. Since it was trained on past resume submissions, mostly from men, the tool learned to unfairly penalize resumes containing the word "women's" or from all-female colleges. The company had to stop using the project in 2017 because it couldn't fix the gender bias.
- **AI Lack of Transparency**: German journalists uncovered a 2021 investigation revealing that an AI-powered video interviewing platform generated biased personality scores based on unrelated factors. A candidate's score could be manipulated simply by adjusting their accessories, hairstyle, or background setting, showing that the AI was swayed by superficial details rather than actual qualifications.

[12] https://www.bbc.com/travel/article/20240222-air-canada-chatbot-misinformation-what-travellers-should-know

- **AI Lack of Transparency**: According to a 2022 review, AI algorithms used to diagnose skin diseases often lack transparency and provide insufficient information about the data sets they're based on, including racial and ethnic diversity. This lack of transparency raises concerns about biased diagnostic recommendations, as an AI trained mostly on images of lighter skin tones may provide less accurate diagnoses for patients with darker skin tones.

The risks from AI are not just theoretical; they are already becoming real-world issues that organizations are having to manage. The above examples are just a few of the ones made public in a very new technology, and it is only likely to get worse as the use of AI expands and its misuse by bad actors also increases.

Risk

We will start off with two truths: Risk is the possibility of something going wrong, and risk can never be zero. Our world is filled with risk daily. When we walk outside, there is a risk we could get hit by a car or a meteor. But the difference between those two, being hit by a car versus a meteor, is probability. When I walk outside on the sidewalk, it is far more probable I would be struck by a car than a meteor. However, the principle of risk still exists in both: the potentially bad thing to happen, that either a car or a meteor will strike me.

Figure 1-6. *Risk Meter*

The second truth is that risk can never be zero. This is important to understand because, as we identify risks, we must recognize that we cannot eliminate them; we can only reduce the risk. Risk is lowered through mitigation strategies, gathering information before making decisions, diversifying investments or operations, implementing safety protocols, acquiring insurance, developing contingency plans, and fostering a culture of risk awareness through training and communication.

There are four main methods to mitigate risk, and they are Avoidance, Reduction, Transfer, and Acceptance.

Avoidance

Avoiding an activity is an effective way to reduce risk. This method reduces exposure to the risk by not engaging in the activity that poses it. Every risk management program and strategy should include this as an option. However, it is rarely used in practice because many activities cannot be avoided or simply not performed. Because of this, avoidance is most often employed when there is a high likelihood of the risk occurring and a significant impact on the organization. Additionally, when the potential costs are high, avoidance appears to be the most cost-effective choice. For example, a bank might avoid giving loans to individuals with a high history of defaults.

Reduction

The reduction of risk, even minimally, is most often the outcome expected when risk is discovered. Implementing solid and strategic risk control measures to mitigate and lower potential risks before they become issues is the key to risk reduction. Most often, examples of this risk reduction in practice are when Multi-Factor Authentication (MFA) is enforced for privileged access accounts due to their high risk for both attack and impact if breached. The reduction activity is most often used in operational activities when risks can be controlled through other compensating activities.

Transfer

Transferring the risk to another party is often done by obtaining insurance, such as cyber-liability insurance, in case of a breach or incident. Moving the risk from your plate or risk register lowers the risk to near zero for your team, but not completely zero. For example, if you buy cyber-liability insurance for a breach and the insurance covers your direct losses, it will not cover reputational losses (mostly because they are near impossible to calculate). Even in this case, risk is not zero. Risk transfer is most often done when there is a high potential for an issue to happen but low probability that it will happen due to compensating controls that are in place.

Acceptance

Risk is usually accepted if it falls outside of an organization's mitigation time frame standards. For example, if an organization has a high risk, which must be mitigated within 30 days, and requires a detailed action plan to reduce the risk, then the risk can be accepted for the time frame necessary to implement the mitigation strategies. If it is a high enough risk, then secondary controls should be put in place to monitor the risk as steps are taken to mitigate the risk. When risk is accepted, the organization must have a formal approval process for the acceptance of the risk. There must also be a risk register that tracks and regularly reviews the accepted risks. The accepted risks must also have a deadline or due date for these reviews; it must not be "open-ended" with no date for re-evaluation. When accepted risks do not have a re-evaluation date, then they are usually forgotten about and can metastasize.

There are a few other ways that risk can be managed that are not as common as the four listed above, but are beneficial to discuss. The first is Risk Sharing, where your business partners or vendors share the risk or distribute the risk across multiple teams or organizations. The key to success in this instance is a clear legal agreement, and establishing communication methods early. This is most often used in joint ventures where business partners share in the risks and rewards. Another example is between your organization and cloud service providers, in which you participate in a shared responsibility model.

Risk buffering is an instance when critical systems requiring high availability will add extra resources, scheduling, or personnel to lessen the risk. Another way to buffer is to implement redundant servers or backup systems to reduce the risk of failure. Risk strategizing is when complex projects with multiple points of failure are injected with contingency plans for specific risks. Risk diversification is the action of spreading potential risks across various projects, products, or businesses to reduce impact or risk exposure.

How to Measure

There are two main ways to measure risk: quantitatively and qualitatively. Qualitative risk analysis is a method for evaluating risks by subjectively rating their probability and impact of occurring on a sliding scale (1–5 or low to high). This helps quickly prioritize risks for organizations by using expert judgment to identify potential threats or opportunities.

Impact →

Likelihood ↑	Negligible	Minor	Moderate	Significant	Severe
Very Likely	Low Med	Medium	Med Hi	High	High
Likely	Low	Low Med	Medium	Med Hi	High
Possible	Low	Low Med	Medium	Med Hi	Med Hi
Unlikely	Low	Low Med	Low Med	Medium	Med Hi
Very Unlikely	Low	Low	Low Med	Medium	Medium

Figure 1-7. *Risk Matrix*

Qualitative risk analysis relies on subjective judgment that is based upon the knowledge and experience of subject-matter experts to rate the risks. It is often viewed as a quicker option, which makes it faster to perform and less data-intensive compared to a quantitative method. There is a focus on risk prioritization, with the primary goal of quickly identifying and ranking risks to help teams decide which ones to focus on first. It is most often used when there is a lack of mathematical or statistical data points available. The other advantage is that data necessary to perform qualitative analysis is quick and easy to obtain and understand. In order to leverage this methodology, you first need to identify your risks. Next, you need to assess the probability of the risk occurring, followed by the impact of it occurring. Last, you can determine the level of risk by plotting your impact and likelihood on a risk matrix (as in Figure 1-2). The risk matrix should be aligned with your organization's risk appetite.

The biggest challenge with this methodology is that it is prone to human bias. For example, let's say your organization classifies a specific risk as High. Compared to what? Your immediate response would be to compare it to medium and low risks. That may be correct, but it is still a rather arbitrary designation that is not backed by any repeatable, measurable standard.

The next person who performs the analysis is likely to classify the risk in a different way, using their own bias. You can reduce the bias of the qualitative method by ensuring your organization's risk rating methodology is well defined and transparent, and that it aligns with your organization's risk appetite (or the risk your organization is willing to accept).

The other method of measuring risk is quantitative risk analysis. Quantitative Risk Analysis (QRA) uses data-driven, scenario-based methods to express risk in measurable terms, often financial. Instead of relying on subjective ratings, a quantitative approach breaks risk into its underlying components (such as the frequency of threat events and the magnitude of potential losses). It then uses calibrated estimates to model how a risk scenario could unfold. Techniques like probability distributions and Monte Carlo simulations are applied to generate a range of possible outcomes, enabling organizations to understand the variability and probable financial impact of a loss event. Although quantitative analysis requires structured data and analytical expertise, it delivers a more objective and defensible view of risk exposure compared to qualitative assessments. An example of output from this type of analysis is noted below:

- There is a 25% probability of a breach in the next five years with an impact of $5M.

Notice there is a probability statement added to this sentence. This is an important distinction with the qualitative methodology, which gives nebulous Low, Medium, and High more meaning. A percentage like 25% can be used in a math formula to determine how much risk over the next five years an organization is exposed to. This calculation can also make it easier for organizations to obtain cyber-liability insurance that covers the overhang.

There are some key steps in this methodology. First, similar to the qualitative approach, you will identify the risks. An additional step is to then gather objective, measurable data for each identified risk. There are some options for performing risk quantification:

- **Expected Monetary Value (EMV)**: A simple quantitative technique where the expected outcome is calculated by multiplying the probability of an event by its estimated financial impact. EMV is most appropriate for discrete, one-time events with well-defined probabilities, but it is not typically used for complex, variable risks such as cyber or operational risk.
- **Three-Point Estimate**: A technique that uses "optimistic," "pessimistic," and "most likely" values to estimate a range of possible outcomes and calculate an expected value. This method helps account for uncertainty by incorporating multiple possible results rather than relying on a single point estimate.
- **Monte Carlo Simulation**: A quantitative modeling technique that applies probability distributions to uncertain inputs and runs many simulations to generate a full spectrum of possible outcomes. Monte Carlo analysis provides a probabilistic view of risk exposure rather than a single deterministic estimate.
- **Decision Tree Analysis**: A structured, visual method for mapping decision options, associated risks, and potential costs or benefits. Decision trees evaluate different paths and their probabilities to support selecting the option with the most favorable expected outcome.

Once a quantitative method has been selected, the analysis phase applies mathematical models to evaluate the data and determine the organization's overall risk exposure, including the range and likelihood of future impacts. Quantitative approaches offer several advantages, the most significant being the ability to support better-informed decision-making. Because the results are expressed in financial terms rather than subjective ratings such as High, Medium, or Low, the analysis provides leaders with clearer, more actionable insights. This level of precision enhances the effectiveness of risk reporting and strengthens alignment between risk management and business objectives. It is recommended that this methodology be used when sufficient data is available to support the analysis. In the past, there was a perception, particularly in areas such as cybersecurity and AI, that the necessary data did not exist to conduct meaningful quantitative assessments. However, this is no longer the case. Today, extensive datasets and industry research provide ample information to support robust, data-driven risk modeling.

Risk-Based Approach

Not all risks are created equal. As your organization identifies, measures, and mitigates risk, it is important to remember that whichever methodology you choose to determine risk level (Quantitative or Qualitative), your team decides how many resources to commit. For lower-risk situations, you would ideally spend less time and resources. In our profession, it can be tempting for risk management professionals to try to be superheroes and fix all problems by managing every risk. However, that is not best practice, not wise, and regulators do not expect it. There should be a direct relationship between risk level and the effort spent on it. High risk should mean a high amount of time and resources, while low risk means less time and energy. Whether it's AI, cyber, or privacy risk, always adopt a risk-based approach.

Third-Party Risk

Let's first define third party. A third party is any person, group, or entity that provides products or services to an organization and operates outside the organization's direct control.. In business, this could be a vendor, supplier, partner, consultant, etc. There does not have to be a monetary exchange or contract in place for an individual or organization to be considered a third party. Also, the term third party is synonymous with vendor.

Third-party risk is the potential negative effect on an organization's data, finances, operations, or reputation caused by the actions or inactions of a third party, such as a vendor, supplier, partner, or contractor. This risk can potentially result in data breaches, financial losses, operational disruptions, reputational harm, and regulatory fines, as organizations are ultimately accountable for the security and compliance of their entire supply chain.

Third-party risk management (TPRM) involves systematically identifying, assessing, monitoring, and mitigating risks from external vendors, suppliers, partners, and service providers. An effective TPRM program enables organizations to proactively manage third-party risks through systematic due diligence, ongoing oversight, and data analysis to lessen the impact of disruptions and safeguard business interests.

Primer

Most would consider current TPRM best practice as a program and process that has been around for well over ten years, when the Finance space was given the regulatory requirement from the Office of the Comptroller of the Currency (OCC) in the United States. Our previous books, *Cybersecurity & Third-Party Risk* and *Zero-Trust & Third-Party Risk*, cover this topic in detail; however, we will provide an overview to ensure all readers are on the same page and understand how risk identification, assessment, and management are conducted.

TPRM Life Cycle

The third-party risk management life cycle has six components as defined by Third Party Risk Association (TPRA). These six components are not cyclical and have a beginning and an end.

1. Governance and Oversight
2. Pre-Contract Due Diligence
3. Contract Review
4. Continuous Monitoring
5. Disengagement
6. Continuous Improvement

Figure 1-8. *TPRM Life Cycle*

Governance and oversight is the first phase because it is the most important, as it lays out the foundations for the TPRM program to build upon. In this phase, the organization has taken the steps to document TPRM policies and procedures, communicate roles and responsibilities, ensure compliance with program expectations, and budget for all aspects of the program. It includes all the pre-work that is required to ensure TPRM work is done correctly and consistently.

Pre-Contract is the phase where TPRM and other key stakeholders begin to identify risks in a potential vendor relationship. During this phase, the teams start processing the vendor intake. A profile is created in the system of record for vendors (if one does not already exist), and the Inherent Risk Assessment (IRA) is conducted. The IRA consists of a series of strategic questions designed to identify which risk areas need further due diligence and care. It is crucial that the IRA serves as a trigger for risk assessments, rather than conducting actual due diligence through this questionnaire. Ideally, most IRQs will contain ten to 20 questions, with a few exceptions. As part of this process, practitioners determine which risk assessments to deploy based on the risk domains triggered within the IRQ. Risk assessments are then conducted to determine the residual risk (or the risk remaining after controls have been evaluated).

The easiest analogy for residual risk versus inherent risk is to use an automobile. At first glance, without any prior examination, a car is inherently high risk. However, if you buy a brand new car with all the features, it has a lot of controls in place to reduce the risk and impact of an accident. Seatbelts, supplemental restraints, automatic braking, blind spot warnings, and more all make a brand new car's residual risk lower than its inherent risk.

Contract review is a separate phase because it serves as a critical milestone in most vendor relationships. Once the contract is signed, your ability or leverage to ask the vendor to change any terms, update security controls, or ask for additional information or assessment work is significantly reduced. Additionally, certain terms in a contract need careful consideration. Some important items to include in any vendor contract are incident notification, encryption for all data, and the ability to perform a security assessment.

Once a contract is signed, the third party enters the Continuous Monitoring phase. When a vendor is onboarded, the risks and threats do not stop; therefore, it is necessary to continue to track third parties with significant risk throughout their entire life cycle. Continuous monitoring involves using various tools (vendor reputation tools, cyber threat tools, SIEM tools, etc.) to detect potential risks associated with higher-risk vendors. After these risks are identified, the team follows up to ensure those issues are resolved.

Disengagement is the process of offboarding a vendor when the relationship ends. Those in the TPRM profession will know that we don't seem to disengage from vendors as often as we onboard them. This often causes many teams to not perform this phase very well or at all. During this phase, teams should focus on ensuring that the data the vendor has for your organization is destroyed or returned, and that all connections and access are removed or closed. Checklists are helpful in this phase to prevent teams from missing important steps in the offboarding process.

Lastly, the Continuous Improvement phase is more of a foundation supporting all other phases than a stand-alone stage to complete after Disengagement. The statement "There is always room for improvement" is true, and it is crucial for your program to have a way to generate and utilize feedback for ongoing improvement. In addition, it is important to continuously review emerging risks or regulations and update your program to ensure it covers the emerging risks or regulations.

Third-party risk management is a well-established field with ample documentation on how to effectively design and implement a program. Aside from this author's earlier works, there are associations and online forums where practitioners engage to learn and grow in this area.

Risk-Based Approach

As you identify, assess, and mitigate any risk, it is important to always keep a "risk-based approach" as your strategy. Not all risks are created equal, and a low-risk vendor should not get the same amount of due diligence and due care that a medium or high-risk vendor would need. Regulators worldwide support and promote a risk-based approach, which involves identifying, assessing, and prioritizing the most critical risks to concentrate resources on mitigating them.[13] This strategy replaces a prescriptive,

[13] https://pmc.ncbi.nlm.nih.gov/articles/PMC4950452/#:~:text=The%20central%20conceit%20of%20risk,proportionate%20(Rothstein%2C%202006).

one-size-fits-all approach with a more efficient and adaptable system that enables businesses to customize due diligence efforts based on their specific risk environments, ultimately improving compliance and resource use for both regulators and the regulated entities.

It allows regulators to concentrate their limited resources on activities that pose the greatest potential harm or risk to achieving regulatory goals, rather than attempting to prevent all possible risk. By focusing on high-risk areas, regulations become more effective and proportional to actual threats, resulting in better outcomes. This approach recognizes that businesses vary, and a one-size-fits-all, prescriptive approach is not suitable for everyone. Lastly, it promotes a clearer understanding between regulators and regulated entities about risks and necessary mitigation strategies. Of course this strategy is also important for less regulated industries as well.

It is common for folks in any risk management role to want to solve all risks and issues. That is not recommended, expected, or best practice. Look to use a risk-based approach as you manage resources by leveraging your organization's risk appetite.

Frameworks

There are currently two frameworks available to help organizations structure their third-party risk management programs. Frameworks are critically important for a few key reasons. First, they ensure nothing is overlooked. Designed to be comprehensive and complete, following a framework for program design and implementation can guarantee that no important controls or risks are left out of the final product. Without a framework, your program becomes a "bucket of best practices." Second, a framework offers a way for your program to evolve and improve. These frameworks are updated as threats and risks change over time, allowing your program to incorporate these vital updates as they occur. Overall, frameworks are a very useful tool when designing or evaluating your existing program.

TPRA TRPM 101 Guidebook

The first framework is from the Third Party Risk Association and their "Third Party Risk Management 101 Guidebook,"[14] which is free to download. The TPRA Framework is a community-sourced e-book that provides an excellent guide to designing, implementing, and enhancing a third-party risk management program. The first edition was published in 2023 and provides for all the phases and processes required to design and run a successful TPRM program. TPRA breaks the process very similarly to what was described above:

- Program Planning and Oversight (PPO)
- Pre-Contract Due Diligence (PCDD)
- Contract Review (CR)
- Continuous Monitoring (CM)
- Disengagement (D)
- Continuous Program Improvement (CPI)

The acronyms at the end of each phase are important as they break out the framework into control best practices that are tracked by their acronyms and numbering. For example, on Continuous Monitoring (CM), there are five sub-categories listed as

- Continuous Monitoring (CM)
- CM 1 - Ongoing Monitoring
- CM 2 - Site Visits

[14] https://www.tprassociation.org/guidebook

- CM 3 - Triggered (Ad Hoc) Reviews
- CM 4 - Continuous Monitoring Tools
- CM 5 - Continuous Metrics and Reporting

In the guidebook, each sub-category includes a detailed description of best practices for that item. The CM 1 - Ongoing Monitoring section begins with an explanation of when this phase starts, followed by the actions expected during this phase (such as ongoing risk assessments), recommendations on how often continuous monitoring should be performed based on residual risk, and what tasks need to be carried out. It covers each phase and sub-category in detail. The guidebook is approximately 147 pages long, including some useful appendices like Helpful Resources, Guidebook Definitions, Best Practices, and more.

This framework is a solid document that benefits the industry and helps ensure that organizations have a complete TPRM program.

Interagency Guidance

The interagency guidance can also serve as a TPRM framework, especially for those in the finance industry. The Office of the Comptroller of the Currency (OCC), the Federal Reserve Board (FRB), and the Federal Deposit Insurance Corporation (FDIC) all came together in June 2023 to issue the "Interagency Guidance on Third-Party Relationships: Risk Management." This was a rare moment of cooperation among agencies, driven by the urgency and risks surrounding third-party issues in the financial sector. The OCC first addressed this years ago, making it a compliance issue for large banks, but now all three agencies are collaborating on their expectations for financial institutions.

The advantage of this regulatory guidance is that it can actually serve as a TPRM framework. It adopts a comprehensive life cycle approach and outlines five phases:

- **Planning**: Assessing risks and benefits of a relationship before it starts.
- **Due Diligence**: Thoroughly evaluating potential third parties.
- **Onboarding**: Structuring the relationship for success.
- **Monitoring**: Continuously assessing risks and performance.
- **Termination**: Efficiently ending relationships while managing potential impacts.

The process is very similar to what is listed by TPRA, and that isn't a coincidence. This five-phase approach (with a continuous improvement phase as a sixth) has been the standard for most mature organizations for some time. The guidance stresses a risk-based approach and advises banks to customize their risk management practices according to the specific risk level and complexity of their relationship with the vendor. Ongoing monitoring is also highlighted as essential, encouraging banks to move beyond annual reviews and adopt more real-time oversight. The risk-based method indicates that this level of attention should be focused on higher-risk third parties.

Because the two examples provided here for frameworks on TPRM are similar (TPRA and the Interagency Guidance), we will use TPRA's phases and program descriptions for the remainder of the book to explain best practices and how to perform actions in a TPRM program. If your organization does not have a framework selected to backstop your TPRM program, the TPRA or Interagency Guidance are excellent resources to accomplish this important task. If you've already selected one of these as a TPRM framework, then many of the activities your program performs should be covered by this book.

Frameworks

Supply chain risk management is a systematic way to pinpoint, evaluate, reduce, and track potential disruptions in a supply chain. The goal is to keep operations running smoothly and ensure a reliable flow of goods and services. This involves pinpointing vulnerabilities, analyzing their potential impact, creating strategies to minimize risk, putting those strategies into action, and continually monitoring their effectiveness. Key components include risk governance, clear communication, and strategies like working with multiple suppliers and having backup logistics plans in place to build resilience. Several frameworks are available for supply chain risk management. The NIST RMF is flexible and can be applied to supply chains, while ISO 31000 offers another option.

For cyber supply chain risk management (C-SCRM), frameworks are most suitable for guiding how to handle the cyber supply chain. Again, NIST RMF or NIST-CSF are flexible enough to address supply chain risks, but the NIST SP 800-161 offers a detailed, risk-based approach specific to C-SCRM that outlines governance for framing, assessing, responding to, and monitoring cyber supply chain risks. Whichever framework is selected, it is crucial to choose and adhere to one. We've previously discussed why frameworks are so important: they help ensure no controls are missed and that, as threats and risks evolve, the framework can guide necessary updates to your programs.

The Convergence

The ongoing AI revolution in software marks a pivotal moment for risk management programs. For years, many programs have struggled with assessing third- and fourth-party vendors due to the vast amounts of data and vendors involved. The speed of threats and vulnerabilities has significantly increased since COVID-19, and geopolitical conflicts are making cyber events, incidents, and breaches more frequent. With the integration of advanced AI solutions into software systems, risk management for TPRM programs has become more complex. However, AI also offers some relief, as it can perform many repetitive tasks that these programs find difficult or cumbersome to manage. The rest of the book will explore these two developments, emphasizing the emergence of robust and capable artificial intelligence.

CHAPTER 2

AI in Vendors

Risk of AI with Vendors

It is no surprise that Artificial Intelligence presents a risk. It is a relatively new concern that TPRM programs are now evaluating and managing, and therefore, some new aspects of that risk need to be explained. AI risks include immediate issues like biased decision-making, privacy violations, and job displacement, as well as long-term existential threats such as loss of human control, potential misuse by malicious actors, and the risk of AI surpassing human intelligence. Other significant risks encompass the spread of misinformation, cybersecurity vulnerabilities, and environmental impacts related to AI's energy use.

Hallucinations

Hallucination in AI refers to when a machine learning model produces outputs that are not based on the input data or factual information. This phenomenon often happens when a model, such as a large language model (LLM), generates responses that sound plausible but are incorrect or nonsensical. As AI systems become more complex, their decision-making processes can quickly become unclear – even to their creators. When the AI faces situations not covered in its training data, unexpected behaviors can occur.

G. C. Rasner, M. C. Rasner, *AI and Third-Party Risk*,
https://doi.org/10.1007/979-8-8688-2465-4_2

An AI hallucination occurs when an AI system generates incorrect, misleading, or unfounded information.

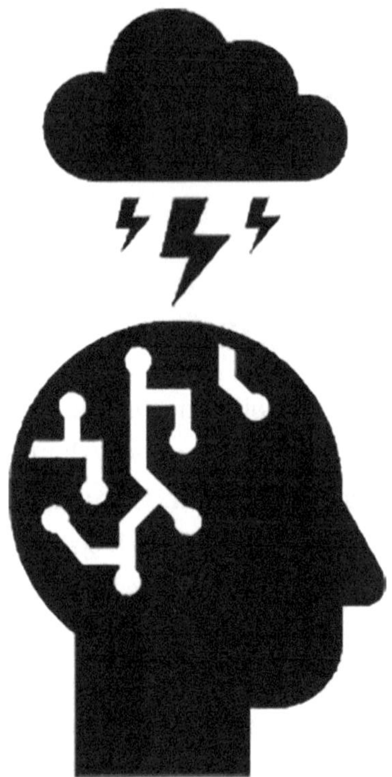

Figure 2-1. *AI Hallucinations*

Hallucinations Risk Management Best Practices

There are a number of ways an organization can lower the risk of hallucinations. One way is to control bias in training data by reviewing and filtering datasets before training or fine-tuning. Owners need to pay close attention to the data to ensure it is not spiked in one direction or another. Human oversight is a key risk control for hallucinations to validate inputs and outputs, especially when the results are used for high-risk projects such as health and safety.

Vendors can also fine-tune the models to ensure alignment with intended goals. Vendors should ensure that exposure is limited for prompt manipulation to ensure only authorized users or systems can perform the prompts and monitor for misuse patterns. Add validations to flag unsupported claims or fabricated outputs and set clear boundaries for model use. Lastly, doing exercises like Threat Modeling for AI will uncover potential edge cases that bad actors may exploit.

Data Privacy Risk

The large amounts of data used to train AI, along with AI's ability to analyze and infer information, pose significant risks to individual and organizational privacy. GenAI systems can unintentionally leak confidential information. This includes personal data, business secrets, or other sensitive inputs used during training.

Data Privacy Risk Management Best Practices

There are ways enterprises can dramatically lower this risk, and they are not new to AI. First is to anonymize sensitive information. There are various techniques to perform anonymization, such as differential privacy, which can be applied to training data to prevent AI from learning or revealing sensitive data. Enforcement of strict access controls to ensure those accessing the data are correct. Regularly test the models for security vulnerabilities and monitoring the AI for external use to detect misuse.

Not unique to AI development, any software should have a secure development life cycle (SDLC) program and process around it. SDLC will ensure that security is implemented into the development of the AI to safeguard against risks from the start of development. Data pathways are another attack point and should be monitored to prevent data leaks. To prevent data leaks, enterprises should be scanning for and detecting sensitive data flowing across the networks.

Lack of Transparency and Explainability

Many advanced AI systems, especially deep learning models, function as black boxes, making it hard to understand or evaluate their decision-making processes. When AI systems make decisions with negative outcomes, it can be unclear who should be held accountable - the developers, the users, or the AI itself? This ambiguity creates challenges for legal and ethical frameworks where accountability is necessary. The "black box" nature of some complex AI systems makes them difficult to understand, leading to issues with transparency, explainability, and determining accountability when things go wrong.

Transparency is about being visible. It's about understanding how the model operates, what data it was trained on, and its limitations. This also involves having access to documentation, performance metrics, and how it handles inputs and outputs. Explainability takes it a step further. It's about understanding the model's decision-making process in a way that makes sense to a human.

When an AI system rejects a loan or flags a health concern, users will naturally want to know the reason. If the system can't provide an explanation, that raises serious operational and ethical concerns. Without transparency, it becomes harder to detect bias. If the model was trained on biased data, it could lead to unfair outcomes. But without understanding how it works, there's no way to audit or fix its behavior. The lack of explainability also makes systems tougher to improve. Developers can't fix what they don't understand. And users may lose trust in the system - especially in high-pressure environments. Some models even memorize parts of their training data, which can be sensitive information that leaks during inference. Without transparency into the model's training process, these risks may go unnoticed.

Unless you understand what the model is doing, you won't be able to secure it, manage it, or expect others to trust it.

Lack of Transparency and Explainability Risk Management Best Practices

The way to lower the risk of this is by documenting every model in use, including its function, training data sources, and known limitations. Make the explanations meaningful and ensure they use business language and help people actually understand what the model is doing. At the root of the explanation, there must be methods included, such as feature importance, natural language justifications, or saliency maps.

Continuously monitor the outputs for bias, drift, or unexpected behaviors that would necessitate a review of the model. Ensure the design is focused on transparency that clarifies what the model can view, what it can output, and where humans are involved for oversight. Loop in the compliance and legal experts to ensure there are no regulatory or legal issues cropping up and avoid black-box explanations from creators.

Adversarial Attack

AI can be used to create new and more sophisticated cyberattacks, and vulnerabilities in AI systems themselves can be exploited to cause harm or gain unauthorized access. AI systems, particularly those based on machine learning, can be susceptible to manipulated inputs designed to deceive them. For instance, subtle alterations to images can cause image recognition systems to make drastically incorrect classifications. There are numerous types of adversarial attacks that warrant explanations:

- **Prompt Injection Attacks**: These attacks manipulate the inputs given to AI systems to make them produce harmful or unintended outputs. They work by embedding malicious instructions in the prompt, which the AI processes as a normal input. As a result, the AI follows the attacker's intent. A prompt can trick an AI into revealing sensitive information or bypassing security measures because many models respond to natural language without proper input validation.
- **Data Poisoning**: Data poisoning is when someone intentionally alters the training data used to create AI models, making them behave in unpredictable or malicious ways. By adding misleading or biased data to the dataset, attackers can manipulate the model's results to favor specific actions or outcomes. This can lead to incorrect predictions, vulnerabilities, or biased decision-making.
- **Access and Authentication Exploits**: These attacks happen when threat actors circumvent or misuse identity controls to get into GenAI systems or the infrastructure that supports them. Since AI often links to internal data, production APIs, and external services, if attackers gain access, they don't just see data they can also alter models, outputs, and downstream systems. Most GenAI setups involve APIs, web services, and integrations across storage, inference engines, databases, and front-end apps. These are secured with credentials, such as tokens, secrets, or service accounts. If any of these are compromised, attackers can impersonate legitimate users or services.

- **Insecure AI-generated code**: AI-generated code is used to save time and money. Many see it as a shortcut to faster development and no downside in quality. Of course, that's not always how it turns out. These tools can create a serious security risk, and many developers may not even be aware of it.
- **AI Worm**: AI worms represent an emerging form of malware that ingeniously employs artificial intelligence to facilitate their proliferation and data theft. Unlike conventional malware, which exploits vulnerabilities within code, an AI worm manipulates AI models to generate seemingly innocuous text or images that conceal malicious code. The recent development known as "Morris II" AI worm functions through adversarial self-replicating prompts techniques that deceive AI systems into producing responses embedded with malicious code. When users respond to these compromised messages, such as replying to an email, their devices may become infected. This innovative methodology complicates detection efforts and enhances the difficulty of maintaining effective protection against such threats. Although Morris II currently exists solely as a research endeavor within controlled environments, it underscores potential security vulnerabilities as AI systems become increasingly interconnected. Experts caution that developers and organizations must proactively address these vulnerabilities, particularly given the growing autonomy of AI assistants in executing tasks on behalf of users.

Adversarial Attack Risk Management Best Practices

This area of risk and threat has some simple but important best practices to lower the risks and threats. First is to ensure there is a secure development life cycle (SDLC), so secure by design is part of the infrastructure for development of any product, especially AI. Make sure the developers understand that code isn't secure unless it follows this process. You also want to ensure developers have training specific to the risks around code development and AI risks, such as bias and data privacy.

Another key piece to ensure reduced risk is not to trust the AI outputs without question. Treat any output from AI like you would a developer-in-training and review the work. Until there is a sense that the AI is really getting it 100% right all the time over a specific period of time, the output should be questioned and checked regularly. Use multiple methods to check the output, as no tool is perfect.

Least privileged access should be applied to any AI model. Specific controls around least privileged include, but are not limited to: implementing role-based access (RBAC) to ensure only those who require access get that access; isolating models from environments that contain sensitive data; restricting any other access to the model (e.g., API) to read-only if possible; and ensuring the identity and access management (IAM) and privileged access management (PAM) programs are well-governed.

A strong defense is also necessary to reduce this risk. Vulnerability management, threat detection, and other cybersecurity practices must ensure they are well-organized programs that address AI-related risks. Conduct simulated attacks to practice team responses, reducing confusion during real incidents. Train models to identify malicious data using adversarial training and real-time input classifiers to enhance detection. This is most effectively achieved through reinforcement learning with human feedback.

Lastly, solid governance around how an organization manages AI risks, development, and security/privacy is key to success. Set boundaries for which AI tools and services can be used, as well as how and what data can be leveraged by an AI model. Define AI governance roles for policy creation and compliance enforcement. Have a process defined for how assessments are performed and use a sandbox for testing, if possible, prior to production deployment. Ensure there is a system to detect rogue AI use within an organization and maintain continuous oversight.

Figure 2-2. *Inspect the AI*

Data Manipulation or Poisoning

Artificial intelligence can be used to create and spread false or misleading information, including deepfakes, which can shape public opinion, erode shared understanding, and intensify social divisions. Data poisoning is when someone intentionally alters the data used to train AI models, making them behave in unexpected or malicious ways. By sneaking in biased or misleading data, attackers can skew the model's results to promote certain actions or outcomes. This can lead to flawed predictions, security vulnerabilities, or biased decision-making.

Data Manipulation Risk Management Best Practices

Methods for reducing the risk of manipulation or poisoning is to have a secure development life cycle (SDLC) that includes the security of the software supply chain. This should cover models, databases, and any data source that is involved in the development. Secure the data pathways by understanding how data moves through the AI system; once there is an understanding of how data flows, any potential risk should be examined with a threat modeling exercise to find threats. Strong identity and access processes are important here as well to ensure no unauthorized access. Establish a process to detect anomalies in the data that would be indicative of poisoning or manipulation.

Bias

AI systems can perpetuate and even amplify existing societal biases present in their training data, resulting in unfair or discriminatory outcomes in areas such as hiring, credit, and criminal justice.

Bias Risk Management Best Practices

To reduce AI model bias, use diverse and representative training data, implement fairness-aware algorithms, regularly conduct bias audits, and adopt explainable AI (XAI) for transparency. Additionally, build a diverse and ethically trained AI development team, establish clear AI governance, and utilize tools like synthetic data, bias detection, and monitoring to sustain ongoing fairness. Train AI models on datasets that reflect the diversity of the intended user population, including various demographics and geographic regions, to prevent skewed results. If demographic gaps exist in real-world datasets, use synthetic data to ensure comprehensive representation and avoid sampling bias.

Use algorithms and tools that can rebalance biased datasets or adjust model results during training to lower unfair impacts. Incorporate fairness metrics (like demographic parity or equalized odds) into the model development and evaluation process. Regularly conduct audits with specialized tools (e.g., Google's What-If Tool or IBM's AI Fairness 360) to identify new biases as models evolve. Create formal governance structures, including clear documentation and audit trails, as part of the machine learning life cycle to manage and address biases. Deploy automated monitoring and data observability tools to detect anomalies and measure bias and fairness metrics in real-world settings.

Scalability and Malfunctions

AI systems can fail due to bugs, data inconsistencies, or unforeseen interactions with their environment. In critical applications like autonomous vehicles or medical diagnosis, such failures could have severe consequences. Also, AI models that perform well in controlled environments may fail when scaled up to real-world applications or when faced with novel situations. Ensuring robustness across diverse scenarios remains a significant challenge.

Scalability and Malfunctions Risk Management Best Practices

Many of the same recommendations made to lower the risk would work equally well in this space. Ensuring a solid SDLC to have security built in from the design. Governance that deals with all the aspects and life cycle of AI is critical to lowering this risk. Lastly, proper capacity planning so that as a model's use is expanded, scalability doesn't become an issue.

Shadow AI

Shadow AI refers to employees or vendors using AI tools without proper oversight or governance. These unauthorized tools pose a risk to your organization's privacy and network security, and can also lead to compliance issues. This behavior is similar to "Shadow IT" and "Shadow SaaS" actions by business partners who don't follow the process or avoid it to get things done. Employees might use external AI tools to summarize meetings, write emails, or generate code. Although their intentions are usually harmless, these tools can accidentally process sensitive data, like customer information, intellectual property, or internal communications without proper safeguards in place.

When these tools are used outside of formal review and procurement channels, no one checks whether they meet the organization's security, compliance, or privacy standards. This leads to blind spots. Since security and IT teams often don't have visibility into which tools are being used or what data they're accessing, this lack of oversight makes it tough to track data movement, prevent data leaks, or enforce controls. It also increases the risk of exposure through insecure AI workflows or poor data handling practices.

Figure 2-3. *AI in the Shadows*

Shadow AI puts the organization's security at risk by enabling AI adoption without the necessary governance and risk controls. As AI becomes more ingrained in daily work, it's crucial to address these gaps proactively. If not, AI usage will outpace the organization's ability to manage the associated risks.

Shadow AI Risk Management Best Practices

Organizations must have established a clear AI use policy and set boundaries for when and how the tools can be utilized. Explain what types of data are acceptable to use and how AI services are to be evaluated. Monitoring for unauthorized use must be done across users, devices, and networks, and maintaining continuous oversight with real-time monitoring tools to keep pace with the potential sprawl. Governance and oversight must be clearly established and published with directions about how formal risk assessments are performed prior to adoption.

AI presents risks like prompt injection, data poisoning, insecure code, model drift, content bias, shadow AI, and data leakage. These affect security, privacy, trust, and compliance throughout the AI life cycle. Implement access controls, input validation, code reviews, behavior monitoring, data protection, and strong governance policies. Regular audits and human oversight are essential at every stage of the AI life cycle.

How to Assess AI Risk in a Vendor

As the book begins with the statement "AI is just another risk" (with some qualifications about its complexity and lack of transparency), the focus is on how to identify risks, evaluate them, and then mitigate them as close to zero as possible. The earlier sections of the book outlined the fundamentals of risk, TPRM, AI, and the dangers linked to Artificial Intelligence. Now, we will explain how organizations can evaluate the risk of AI developed or leveraged by third parties.

Frameworks: Why and Which

Why are frameworks discussed so often, and why are they so crucial? Without frameworks, there's no guarantee that your program or process will cover all the known control areas and risks. In fact, it's nearly certain that some will be overlooked, turning your program or process into a mere "bucket of best practices." Not a flattering description. Additionally, a framework ensures that as threats and risks evolve - something they do constantly - your program or process can be updated in tandem with the framework.

Frameworks are an important part of any AI assessment because one of the first steps to success in AI development and deployment is solid governance. As you begin to look at an AI vendor for assessment, knowing what framework they use and how they use it will help your team understand their security and maturity level. Also, as your own organization adopts AI solutions, it will also need to either adopt an AI framework or take an existing risk management framework (RMF) it currently uses and map the AI risks to it. For example, while it is preferable to use the NIST AI RMF, it is possible to use NIST-CSF 2.0 to manage AI risks with a little bit of extra mapping effort.

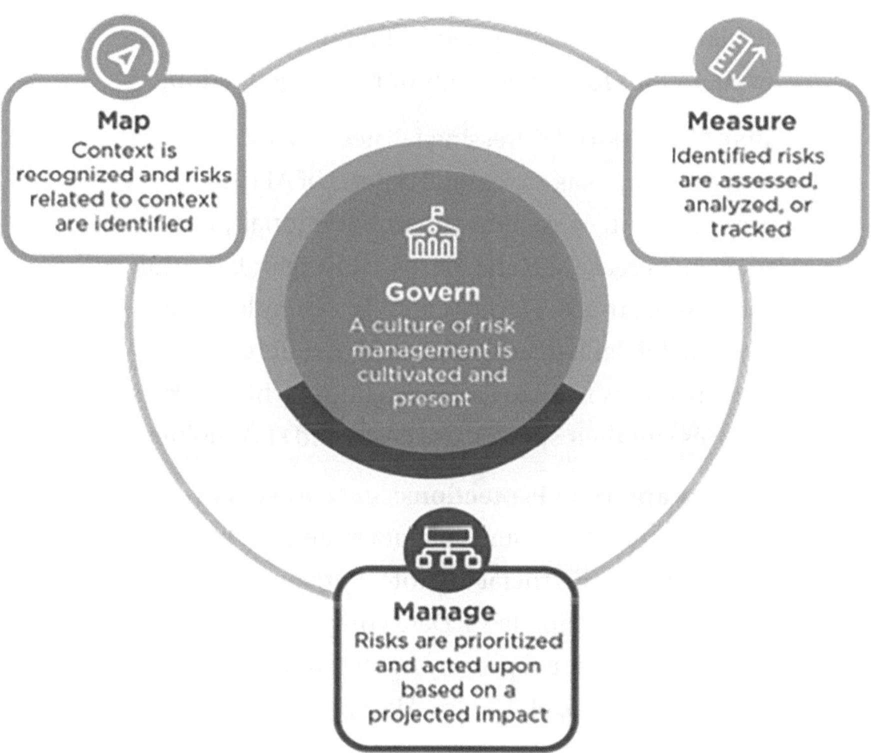

Figure 2-4. *AI Frameworks*

Key Elements of an AI Risk Framework

There are seven key elements of an AI risk framework to be complete and accurate. Some of these elements have been discussed in earlier sections, but bear repeating due to their risk and relevance.

- **Governance**: The most effective risk management programs start and operate with rock-solid governance models and clear lines of responsibility and accountability.
- **Transparency and Explainability**: Transparency involves being open about the data used, the algorithms applied, and the system's limitations. Explainability takes it a step further by providing clear explanations for AI decisions or recommendations.
- **Bias Mitigation**: Addressing fairness issues and reducing bias are essential parts of AI risk management. AI systems can unintentionally reinforce or even increase societal biases, causing unfair results for certain groups. Fairness in AI is a complex idea that can be defined and measured in different ways. Organizations need to carefully choose which fairness metrics suit their specific use cases and stakeholders.
- **Privacy and Data Protections**: Since AI systems often depend on large amounts of data, including personal information, it is crucial to protect privacy and comply with data protection laws. Data compliance aims to safeguard individual privacy rights while allowing the beneficial use of data for AI development and deployment.

- **Security Controls**: AI systems face security threats such as data poisoning, model inversion attacks, and adversarial examples. Implementing security measures is crucial to protect AI systems from malicious actors and ensure their dependable operation.
- **Human Oversight**: While AI systems can provide powerful capabilities, maintaining proper human oversight and control is necessary to manage risks and ensure accountability. This part of the framework emphasizes finding the right balance between AI autonomy and human judgment.
- **Continuous Monitoring**: Due to the ever-changing nature of AI technologies and their operating environments, ongoing oversight and enhancement of AI systems' performance, impacts, and emerging risks are vital components of an AI risk management framework.

AI Risk Management Frameworks

There are a few major AI risk management frameworks, despite the relative newness of the technology stack. We will take a look at a few of them but spend most of the time on the NIST AI RMF 1.0 due to its relative popularity and because it can easily be "translated" into other frameworks and languages, given the online resources around it.

NIST AI Risk Management Framework (AI RMF 1.0)

An AI Risk Management Framework (AI RMF) is a set of guidelines and processes for handling the risks related to AI systems, with the NIST-AI RMF being a leading example. The NIST AI RMF is intended for voluntary use by developers, users, and evaluators to identify, evaluate, and reduce risks across the AI life cycle from design and development to deployment and use to encourage trustworthy and responsible AI. It is organized around four core functions: Govern, Map, Measure, and Manage, which work together in an ongoing cycle for improvement and to build trust in AI technologies.

The NIST AI Risk Management Framework is built around four functions that guide continuous risk management. First is Govern, which establishes the AI risk management culture and process within the organization, ensuring senior leadership's awareness and commitment. Second is Map, where the team works to understand the context in which the AI system is being used, identifying potential risks, harms, and trust characteristics throughout the AI life cycle. Measure, the third function, evaluates the risks by developing and applying measures to the AI risks, allowing for the measurement and characterization of the AI system outcomes, and ensuring trustworthiness. Lastly is Manage, where action is taken to address risks by prioritizing and responding to risks, allocating resources, and making changes to mitigate the identified risks.

The NIST AI RMF begins by defining three categories of harm that users need to evaluate. Harm to People is addressed first, focusing on protecting individual liberties, ensuring freedom from physical or psychological harm, and promoting equal opportunities while supporting democracy and education. Harm to an Organization involves protecting against operational disruptions, potential risks from breaches, and damage to reputation. Finally, Harm to an Ecosystem aims to prevent sector or supply chain disruptions and reduce environmental and natural resource damage.

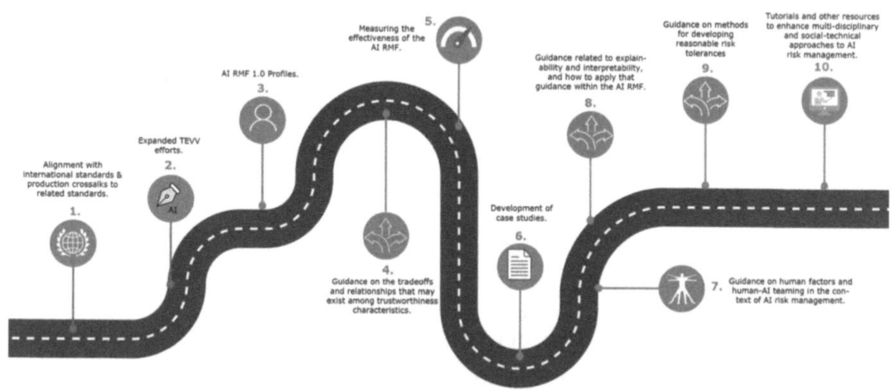

Figure 2-5. *AI Roadmap from NIST AI RMF*

To assist organizations in avoiding these three types of harms, the Risk Management Framework outlines seven essential characteristics of trustworthy AI systems:

1. **Valid and Reliable**: AI systems should produce accurate and dependable results. If the system's results are not accurate or dependable, then, as the first characteristic, the AI system is already failing.

2. **Safe**: Artificial Intelligence systems should prioritize user safety and prevent harm. After producing valid and reliable results, the system must be safe for the operator and the public. See the three Categories of AI Harm to understand the scope of this characteristic.

3. **Secure and Resilient**: AI systems should defend against malicious attacks and remain resilient when facing challenges. This characteristic can be described best as "Secure by Design," and the creators thought of security while designing the system, so it starts off safe and secure.

4. **Accountable and Transparent**: Artificial Intelligence systems should be explainable, transparent, and responsible for their decisions. Over complex systems where the creators can't explain in business terms how it was created and managed are ripe for failure. It isn't to say it needs to be simple, but it must be understandable.

5. **Explainable and Interpretable**: The internal workings of AI systems should be understandable and interpretable. While the average user will not be able to "look under the hood" of the AI algorithm and understand it, it should be able to follow a logical workflow and decision tree.

6. **Privacy Enhanced**: Artificial Intelligence systems should respect user privacy and safeguard personal data. AI systems rely on a lot of data, and much of that data can be sensitive and needs to be protected. Ensure any sensitive data is properly managed and secured.

7. **Fair with Harmful Bias Managed**: AI systems should promote fairness in outcomes and actively address harmful biases. Bias is in nearly everything we do as humans, no matter how hard we try to avoid it. It seeps into our work, too, and it can affect AI output as well. Ensuring the AI output is as unbiased as possible is key to success.

NIST AI Risk Management Framework Core Functions

The ability to achieve proper risk management for Artificial Intelligence using the NIST methodology is done with regular evaluations of AI risk. The NIST AI RMF breaks down this continuous risk management process into four categories: Govern, Map, Measure, and Manage.

Figure 2-6. *AI RMF Graphic*

Map is the evaluation section of the process. In the first of the four core functions, the process is to get the diverse teams to provide their perspectives (internal and external), end users, and any impacted teams to list and risk-order the AI risks. Gathering these diverse teams helps alleviate the problem often encountered where AI actors working together on a system do not have visibility or control over the other parts of the model, making it challenging to predict the risks and impacts. In this step of the process, it is about getting a list of all the potential AI risks listed, preferably in risk-ranked order (highest risk to lowest).

Measure takes the AI risks identified and ranked from the Map exercise. Then, AI systems must be tested before deployment and regularly while in operation to maintain a current understanding of their operations and trustworthiness. Teams must consistently analyze, assess, benchmark, and monitor AI risks and impacts through many different tools. Tracking the risks is an important step in this function, and like any other risk in your enterprise, they should be in an Enterprise Risk Register, not in a special place or off to the side, but where all your other risks are stored and tracked.

Manage the AI risks is the third of the core functions. Once your team has Mapped and Measured, then it comes time to Manage the risks. This is accomplished by allocating proper resources to maximize the AI benefits while reducing the risks. This is usually accomplished by taking the risk-ranked list of AI risks and using the risk management techniques we discussed in Chapter 1 (there are four main methods to mitigate risk, and they are Avoidance, Reduction, Transfer, and Acceptance...). If the risk is too great, it could be Avoidance. If the risk has the ability to compensate or mitigate controls, then it can be Risk Reduction. One could transfer the risk by purchasing liability insurance for any potential impact; and lastly, if the risk is low enough of likely impact and rating, then the risk could be accepted, but it must be tracked.

The last core function is really the underlying "base" for the other three: Govern. Governance is a key function in any program as it dictates how it is managed end-to-end. Without Govern, the teams are doing ad hoc and different every time. This core function provides guidelines for the implementation of structures, systems, processes, and teams to ensure a strong risk management culture, a "secure by design" development cycle, and integrated feedback mechanisms. This function underpins the success of Map, Measure, and Manage.

The next step to helping the reader better understand how to leverage this framework is to, at a high level, explain each of the controls in the four core functions, in business language. Along with each of the controls, we can list some potential actions taken to address the risks.

The way the following will work is that it will list the NIST AI RMF Control Number, then a sub-bullet to describe what the organization can do to address the risk or issue. For example:

- *NIST CONTROL X.Y: Control Description from NIST*
- *What the organization can do to lower the risk in business English.*

NIST AI RMF Govern

In this function, controls are focused on policies, processes, procedures, and practices across the organization related to mapping, measuring, and managing AI risks to ensure they are in place, transparent, and effectively implemented.

- **Govern 1.1**: Legal and regulatory requirements around AI are understood, managed, and documented.
    - Organizations must maintain awareness of applicable legal and regulatory requirements and align risk management efforts with applicable legal standards.
- **Govern 1.2**: The characteristics of trustworthy AI are integrated into policies, processes, and procedures.
    - An organization should define key terms and concepts for AI and the scope and purpose of the systems. AI governance is integrated into organizational policies and procedures, not a one-off organization or done ad hoc.
- **Govern 1.3**: Processes and procedures are in place to determine the needed level of risk management activities based on the organization's risk tolerance.

- Companies must have established policies that define mechanisms for measuring or understanding an AI system's impacts and should be integrated into the enterprise risk management framework used by the whole organization.

- **Govern 1.4**: The risk management process and its outcomes are established through transparent policies, procedures, and other controls based on organizational risk priorities.
  - This is best accomplished when organizations have clear policies and procedures relating to documentation and transparency around the Map, Measure, and Manage functions.
- **Govern 1.5**: Ongoing monitoring and periodic review of the risk management process and its outcomes are planned, organizational roles and responsibilities are clearly defined, including determining the frequency of periodic review.
  - An organization should have continuous monitoring in risk management for tracking unexpected issues and performance impacts, in real time or at specific intervals, for AI systems.
- **Govern 1.6**: Mechanisms are in place to inventory AI systems and are resourced according to organizational risk priorities.
  - Organizations must have an AI inventory, and this must be documented and reviewed on a regular basis. Policies must be developed and published that define model usage and how inventories are performed and when.

- **Govern 1.7**: Processes and procedures are in place for the safe and phased decommissioning of AI systems, ensuring that risks are mitigated and the organization's trustworthiness is maintained.
    - Like any system, simply deleting it or removing it without a documented process is not a great idea. There must be a decommissioning process established and followed.
- **Govern 2.0**: Accountability is the focus in this section, by ensuring accountability structures are in place so that appropriate teams and users are empowered, responsible, and trained for Map, Measure, and Manage of AI risks.
- **Govern 2.1**: Roles and responsibilities and lines of communication related to mapping, measuring, and managing AI risks are documented and are clear to individuals and teams throughout the organization.
    - The leadership and organizational structure of the AI teams must be established. Roles and responsibilities should be well-defined.
- **Govern 2.2**: The organization's personnel and partners receive AI risk management training to enable them to perform their duties and responsibilities consistent with related policies, procedures, and agreements.
    - Organizations must identify and integrate training into their enterprise learning requirements based on job role and responsibilities

- **Govern 2.3**: Executive leadership of the organization takes responsibility for decisions about risks associated with AI system development and deployment.
    - Senior leadership must be aware of the AI risks and make informed decisions regarding risk appetite and management of them.
- **Govern 3.0**: This section focuses on diversity, equity, inclusion, and accessibility in how risks are prioritized for AI throughout the life cycle.
- **Govern 3.1**: Decision-making related to mapping, measuring, and managing AI risks throughout the life cycle is informed by a diverse team (e.g., diversity of demographics, disciplines, experience, expertise, and backgrounds).
    - Ensuring the team is diverse (experiences, disciplines, backgrounds, etc.) ensures a better product overall.
- **Govern 3.2**: Policies and procedures are in place to define and differentiate roles and responsibilities for human-AI configurations and oversight of AI systems.
    - There must be policies and procedures that define and differentiate between human roles
- **Govern 4.0**: Focuses on organizational teams that are committed to a culture that considers and communicates AI risk.
- **Govern 4.1**: Organizational policies and practices are in place to foster a critical thinking and safety-first mindset in the design, development, deployment, and use of AI systems to minimize negative impacts.

  - The organization should have policies that require oversight and GRC for AI system design, implementation, and deployment.

- **Govern 4.2**: Organizational teams document the risks and potential impacts of the AI technology they design, develop, deploy, evaluate, and use, and communicate about the impacts more broadly.

  - Organizations should establish impact assessments through policies and procedures for AI systems used and align those assessments with regulatory and legal requirements.

- **Govern 4.3**: Organizational practices are in place to enable AI testing, identification of incidents, and information sharing.

  - A company must have policies and procedures addressing AI system testing, AI system limitations, reporting and documenting incident response, and guidance for information sharing.

- **Govern 5.0**: Ensures processes are in place for robust engagement with relevant AI actors.

- **Govern 5.1**: Organizational policies and practices are in place to collect, consider, prioritize, and integrate feedback from those external stakeholders regarding the potential individual and societal impacts related to AI risks, as developed or deployed by the team.

  - Risk management policies for the organization must address mechanisms for collecting, evaluating, and incorporating feedback.

- **Govern 5.2**: Mechanisms are established to enable AI actors to regularly incorporate adjudicated feedback from relevant AI actors into system design and implementation.
    - Organizations deal with this by defining reasonable risk tolerances for AI systems and allowing for feedback into designs and operations.
- **Govern 6.0**: There is a GRC program, with policies and procedures in place to address AI risks and benefits arising from third-party software and data, and other supply chain issues.
- **Govern 6.1**: Policies and procedures are in place that address AI risks associated with third-party entities, including risks of infringement of a third party's intellectual property or other rights.
    - Does the organization have its own program, like yours, that evaluates the risks of AI coming from vendors and the supply chain?
- **Govern 6.2**: Contingency processes are in place to handle failures or incidents in third-party data or AI systems deemed to be high risk.
    - Does the organization have a documented process in place to deal with outages or interruptions to AI systems?

NIST AI RMF Map

The NIST AI RMF Map function aims to give a complete picture of the AI system's context and potential risks throughout its entire life cycle. This includes pinpointing risks to different stakeholders, evaluating broader socio-technical factors, and outlining the AI system's intended use. By bringing together various internal and external views, the Map function helps organizations put AI system risks into context and lays the groundwork for the next steps in the AI RMF.

- **Map 1.0**: This section is concerned with ensuring context is established and understood for the AI system.
- **Map 1.1**: Intended purpose, potentially beneficial uses, context-specific laws, norms, and expectations, and prospective settings in which the AI system will be deployed are understood and documented. Considerations include specific sets or types of users along with their expectations; potential positive and negative impacts of system use on individuals, communities, organizations, society, and the planet; assumptions and related limitations about AI system purposes; uses and risks across the development or product AI life cycle; TEVV and system metrics.
    - An organization should have awareness of AI trends in industry, technical, and legal standards; there must be a life cycle from development to decommissioning; and the use requirements are well-defined.
- **Map 1.2**: Interdisciplinary AI actors, competencies, skills, and capacities for establishing context reflect demographic diversity and broad domain and user experience expertise, and their participation is documented. Opportunities for interdisciplinary collaboration are prioritized.

    - Ensuring organizations have diversity in their AI ecosystem is important to ensuring better acceptance.

- **Map 1.3**: The organization's mission and relevant goals for the AI technology are understood and documented.
    - What is the organization's level of documentation for AI strategy and outcomes, and are they aligned?
- **Map 1.4**: The business value or context of business use has been clearly defined or, in the case of assessing existing AI systems, re-evaluated.
    - Business value and context should be documented by the organization.
- **Map 1.5**: Organizational risk tolerances are determined and documented.
    - This should be independent of whether they have any AI-enabled systems or products. Every organization must have these documented: risk tolerances. It may be different for AI, but this must be done at all levels for all risk domains as applicable.
- **Map 1.6**: System requirements (e.g., "the system shall respect the privacy of its users") are elicited from and understood by relevant AI actors. Design decisions take socio-technical implications into account to address AI risks.
    - An organization should prioritize trustworthy characteristics in design and system requirements.

- **Map 2.0**: The categorization of the AI system is the focus of this section.
- **Map 2.1**: The specific task and methods used to implement the task that the AI system will support are defined (e.g., classifiers, generative models, recommenders).
    - Organizations should define and document the AI system's existing and potential learning tasks along with known assumptions and limitations.
- **Map 2.2**: Information about the AI system's knowledge limits and how system output may be utilized and overseen by humans is documented. Documentation provides sufficient information to assist relevant AI actors when making informed decisions and taking subsequent actions.
    - There is a lot of documentation required around settings, environments, and conditions that need to be published and managed.
- **Map 2.3**: Scientific integrity and TEVV considerations are identified and documented, including those related to experimental design, data collection, and selection (e.g., availability, representativeness, suitability), system trustworthiness, and construct validation.
    - Identify and document experiment design and statistical techniques that are valid for testing complex socio-technical systems like AI, which involve human factors, emergent properties, and dynamic context(s) of use.

- **Map 3.0**: AI capabilities, targeted usage, goals, and expected benefits and costs are compared with the benchmarks, which are evaluated and understood in this section.
- **Map 3.1**: Potential benefits of intended AI system functionality and performance are examined and documented.
    - Utilize participatory approaches and engage with system end users to understand and document AI systems' potential benefits, efficacy, and interpretability of AI task output.
- **Map 3.2**: Potential costs, including non-monetary costs, which result from expected or realized AI errors or system functionality and trustworthiness, as connected to organizational risk tolerance, are examined and documented.
    - Conduct a context analysis to identify potential negative impacts from not embedding trustworthiness traits. When these impacts are not direct or obvious, AI actors can collaborate with external stakeholders, including impacted communities, to examine and document:
        - Who could be harmed?
        - What could be harmed?
        - When could harm arise?
        - How could harm arise?
    - Identify and establish procedures for regularly assessing the qualitative and quantitative costs of

internal and external AI system failures. Develop actions to prevent, detect, and/or address potential risks and their impacts. Consistently evaluate failure costs to guide go/no-go deployment decisions throughout the AI system's life cycle.

- **Map 3.3**: Targeted application scope is specified and documented based on the system's capability, established context, and AI system categorization.
  - Think about limiting the contexts where the system is deployed, considering factors like: How outcomes might directly or indirectly impact users, groups, communities, and the environment. How long the system is deployed between re-training. The geographical regions it operates in. Community standards and potential for system misuse or abuse (intentional or unintentional). How AI system features and capabilities can be used in other applications or to replace existing processes.
  - Include AI professionals from legal and procurement teams when defining the target application scope.
- **Map 3.4**: Processes for operator and practitioner proficiency with AI system performance and trustworthiness – and relevant technical standards and certifications – are defined, assessed, and documented.
  - Pinpoint and disclose the features and capabilities of AI systems that can impact decision-making by downstream AI actors during deployment and operation. For instance, how certain system

features might trigger known risks in different human-AI interactions, such as selective adherence.

- Identify the specific skills and expertise required for operators, practitioners, and other domain experts who work with AI systems. Create operational guides for AI systems in live and operational settings, detailing known risks, mitigation strategies, and trustworthy features as outlined in Map-1.
- Define and develop training materials for proposed end users, practitioners, and operators about AI system use and known limitations.

- **Map 3.5**: Processes for human oversight are defined, assessed, and documented in accordance with organizational policies from GOVERN function.
    - Identify and document AI systems' features and capabilities that require human oversight, in relation to operational and societal contexts, trustworthy characteristics, and risks identified in MAP-1.
    - Establish practices for AI systems' oversight in accordance with policies developed in GOVERN-1.
    - Define and develop training materials for relevant AI Actors about AI system performance, context of use, known limitations and negative impacts, and suggested warning labels.
- **Map 4.0**: The risks and benefits are mapped for all AI system components, including third-party software and data.

- **Map 4.1**: Approaches for mapping AI technology and legal risks of its components - including the use of third-party data or software - are in place, followed, and documented, as are risks of infringement of a third party's intellectual property or other rights.
    - Examine audit reports, test results, product plans, warranties, terms of service, end user license agreements, contracts, and other documents related to third-party entities to support value assessments and risk management efforts.
    - Review third-party software release schedules and change management plans (hotfixes, patches, updates, forward- and backward-compatibility guarantees) for irregularities that could increase AI system risks.
    - Inventory of third-party materials (hardware, open-source software, foundation models, open-source data, proprietary software, proprietary data, etc.) necessary for system implementation and maintenance.
    - Review redundancies concerning third-party technology and personnel to evaluate potential risks from insufficient support.
- **Map 4.2**: Internal risk controls for components of the AI system, including third-party AI technologies, are identified and documented.
    - Track third parties preventing or hampering risk-mapping as indications of increased risk.

    - Supply resources such as model documentation templates and software safelists to assist in third-party technology inventory and approval activities.
    - Review third-party material (including data and models) for risks related to bias, data privacy, and security vulnerabilities.
    - Apply traditional technology risk controls – such as procurement, security, and data privacy controls – to all acquired third-party technologies.

- **Map 5.0**: Impacts to individuals, groups, communities, organizations, and society are examined and characterized.
- **Map 5.1**: Likelihood and magnitude of each identified impact (both potentially beneficial and harmful) based on expected use, past uses of AI systems in similar contexts, public incident reports, feedback from those external to the team that developed or deployed the AI system, or other data are identified and documented.
    - Create assessment scales to evaluate AI systems' impact. These scales can be qualitative, like red-amber-green (RAG), or involve simulations or econometric methods. Consistently document and apply these scales across the organization's AI portfolio.
    - Identify and document the likelihood and extent of system benefits and negative impacts concerning trustworthiness characteristics.
    - Establish processes for red teaming to identify and link system limitations to AI life cycle stage(s) and potential downstream impacts.

- **Map 5.2**: Practices and personnel for supporting regular engagement with relevant AI actors and integrating feedback about positive, negative, and unanticipated impacts are in place and documented.
    - Set up and document processes for engaging stakeholders early in system development. This helps identify how the AI system might affect individuals, groups, communities, organizations, and society as a whole. Use methods like value-sensitive design (VSD) to pinpoint where organizational and societal values clash with the system's implementation and impact.
    - Identify strategies to engage, gather, and include input from system end users and other key stakeholders to support ongoing monitoring of potential impacts and emerging risks.
    - Incorporate quantitative, qualitative, and mixed methods in assessing and documenting potential impacts on individuals, groups, communities, organizations, and society.
    - Identify an independent team, internal or external, that can evaluate the benefits, positive and negative impacts, and their likelihood of an AI system, separate from AI design and development functions magnitude.
    - Assess and document stakeholder feedback to gauge potential impacts and gather actionable insights on trustworthiness characteristics and design approaches.

NIST AI RMF Measure

One key part of the NIST AI Risk Management Framework (AI RMF) is the Measure function. This involves regularly evaluating and monitoring AI systems to ensure they're trustworthy by looking at their functionality, risks, and impact over time. To do this, the function uses various tools to assess how well AI systems meet the characteristics of trustworthiness, such as reliability, safety, fairness, and transparency. The results provide data to inform decisions about mitigating and managing risks throughout the AI life cycle.

- **Measure 1.0**: In this section, appropriate methods and metrics are identified and utilized.
- **Measure 1.1**: Approaches and metrics for evaluating AI risks identified during the Map function are chosen for implementation, starting with the most critical risks. Risks or trustworthiness characteristics that cannot - or will not - be measured are properly documented.
    - Develop methods for detecting, tracking, and measuring known risks, errors, incidents, or negative impacts.
    - Determine testing procedures and metrics to show whether the system is suitable for its purpose and working as advertised.
    - Determine testing procedures and metrics to demonstrate the effectiveness of the AI system's trustworthiness.
- **Measure 1.2**: Appropriateness of AI metrics and effectiveness of existing controls are regularly assessed and updated, including reports of errors and impacts on affected communities.

    - Evaluate how well measurements made in one setting can be applied to other settings.
    - Regularly assess the effectiveness of existing metrics and controls throughout the AI system's life cycle.
    - Track and document reports of errors, incidents, and negative impacts, and assess whether existing metrics are sufficient and effective for addressing issues and upgrades.

- **Measure 1.3**: Internal experts who did not serve as frontline developers for the system and/or independent assessors are involved in regular assessments and updates. Domain experts, users, AI actors external to the team that developed or deployed the AI system, and affected communities are consulted in support of assessments as necessary per organizational risk tolerance.
    - Use separate testing teams within the Govern function (2.1 and 4.1) to allow for independent decisions and course corrections for AI systems. Monitor processes, measure performance changes, and document the results.
    - Develop and evaluate AI system prototypes with end users early and often throughout the AI life cycle. Record test outcomes and make adjustments as needed.
    - Evaluate the independence and authority of TEVV and oversight AI actors to ensure they have the necessary independence and resources to carry out assurance, compliance, and feedback tasks effectively.

- **Measure 2.0**: AI systems are evaluated for trustworthiness.
- **Measure 2.1**: Test sets, metrics, and details about the tools used during test, evaluation, validation, and verification (TEVV) are documented.
    - Use industry-standard best practices to ensure transparency and thorough documentation of all measurement aspects. This includes creating data sheets for data sets and model cards.
    - Regularly evaluate the effectiveness of tools used to document measurement methods, test sets, metrics, processes, and materials. Update these tools as needed.
- **Measure 2.2**: Evaluations involving human subjects meet applicable requirements (including human subject protection) and are representative of the relevant population.
    - Adhere to human subjects research guidelines set by organizational and disciplinary standards, including obtaining informed consent and providing compensation, during data collection activities.
    - Examine the differences between the intended and actual user populations or data subjects, including the likelihood of errors, incidents, or negative effects.
    - Use disaggregated evaluation methods (e.g., by race, age, gender, ethnicity, ability, region) to enhance AI system performance when deployed in real-world settings.

- **Measure 2.3**: AI system performance or assurance criteria are measured qualitatively or quantitatively and demonstrated for conditions similar to deployment settings. Measures are documented.
    - Engage regularly and consistently with communities that may be affected. Build an internal team that's diverse, multidisciplinary, and collaborative. Continuously test and evaluate systems in less-than-ideal conditions, working closely with AI experts on user interaction and user experience (UI/UX) roles.
- **Measure 2.4**: The functionality and behavior of the AI system and its components - as identified in the MAP function - are monitored when in production.
    - Track and record how metrics and performance indicators in production differ from those collected during pre-deployment testing. When differences arise, consider the risks of error propagation and feedback loops.
    - Use hypothesis testing or expert opinion to assess any differences in the distribution of new input or output data compared to test environments.
    - Keep an eye out for anomalies using methods like control limits, confidence intervals, integrity constraints, and machine learning algorithms. When anomalies are detected, think about the risks of error propagation and the risks of feedback loops.

- **Measure 2.5**: The AI system to be deployed is demonstrated to be valid and reliable. Limitations of the generalizability beyond the conditions under which the technology was developed are documented.
    - Set the operating conditions and socio-technical context for validating the AI system.
    - Create and document processes to determine the system's operational conditions and limits.
    - Determine or identify and document methods to measure various aspects of the system's validity.
- **Measure 2.6**: AI system is evaluated regularly for safety risks – as identified in the MAP function. The AI system to be deployed is demonstrated to be safe; its residual negative risk does not exceed the risk tolerance, and it can fail safely, particularly if made to operate beyond its knowledge limits. Safety metrics implicate system reliability and robustness, real-time monitoring, and response times for AI system failures.
    - Track system performance in real time to quickly respond when AI system incidents occur.
    - Gather key safety data (e.g., out-of-range performance, incident response times, system downtime, injuries, etc.) to potentially share with affected communities or as needed by AI system oversight personnel.
    - Focus measurement on continuous improvement. Aim to expand the range of conditions where the system can fail safely by making system changes based on in-production testing and events.

- **Measure 2.7**: AI system security and resilience - as identified in the MAP function - are evaluated and documented.
  - Set up and monitor AI system security tests and metrics, such as red-teaming activities, the frequency and rate of unusual events, system downtime, response times to incidents, time to bypass security measures, and more.
  - Use red-team exercises to test the system under simulated attack or extreme conditions, measure its response, evaluate potential failure points, and determine if it can recover from unexpected issues.
  - Record the results of red-team exercises as part of ongoing improvement efforts, including the range of security test conditions and results.
- **Measure 2.8**: Risks associated with transparency and accountability - as identified in the MAP function - are examined and documented.
  - Set up the system to measure and track its performance, such as by keeping records of past actions, audit logs, and other data that AI systems can use to identify potential errors, biases, or vulnerabilities. Work closely with experts in user interaction and experience (UI/UX), human-computer interaction (HCI), and human-AI teaming to fine-tune user controls. Test explanations provided by the system with various audiences, including operators, end users, decision-makers, and individuals directly affected by system decisions, to ensure they can understand and challenge the decisions if necessary.

- **Measure 2.9**: The AI model is explained, validated, and documented, and AI system output is interpreted within its context - as identified in the MAP function - and to inform responsible use and governance.
    - Make sure systems are built to produce models with explanations, post hoc explanations, and audit logs. Whenever possible, use methods that are inherently explainable, such as traditional and penalized linear models, decision trees, nearest-neighbor approaches, rule-based models, generalized additive models, explainable boosting machines, and neural additive models. Before deploying, test the explanation methods and the resulting explanations to get feedback from relevant AI experts, end users, and potentially affected individuals or groups on whether the explanations are accurate, clear, and understandable.
- **Measure 2.10**: Privacy risk of the AI system - as identified in the MAP function - is examined and documented.
    - Identify privacy-related values, frameworks, and attributes that are relevant in specific use cases by directly engaging with end users and potentially affected groups.
    - Document how personally sensitive information in datasets is collected, used, managed, and disclosed, following privacy and data governance policies.

    - Measure privacy-level data aspects, such as the ability to identify individuals or groups (e.g., k-anonymity metrics, l-diversity metrics, t-closeness).

- **Measure 2.11**: Fairness and bias - as identified in the MAP function - are evaluated, and results are documented.
    - Carry out fairness evaluations to address both computational and statistical forms of bias.
    - Determine the types of harm that can occur, such as allocational, representational, quality of service, stereotyping, or erasure.
    - Identify the groups that may be harmed, including those that intersect or are within a broader group.
- **Measure 2.12**: Environmental impact and sustainability of AI model training and management activities - as identified in the MAP function - are assessed and documented.
    - Build environmental impact indicators into AI system design and development plans, focusing on reducing consumption and boosting efficiency.
    - Pinpoint and implement key indicators of AI system energy and water usage, efficiency, and/or greenhouse gas emissions.
    - Set measurable baselines for sustainable AI system operation, aligning with organizational policies, regulatory requirements, legal frameworks, and environmental protection and sustainability goals and norms.

- **Measure 2.13**: Effectiveness of the employed TEVV metrics and processes in the MEASURE function is evaluated and documented.
    - Examine the selected system metrics and their corresponding TEVV processes to see if they can support ongoing system improvements, including pinpointing and fixing errors.
    - Regularly assess system metrics for their usefulness and consider simpler descriptive approaches instead of overly complicated methods.
    - Check the selected system metrics to see if they're acceptable to the end users and the communities they affect.
    - Evaluate how well the metrics work in identifying and measuring risks.
- **Measure 3.0**: Mechanisms for tracking AI risks are in place and can be tracked over time.
- **Measure 3.1**: Approaches, personnel, and documentation are in place to regularly identify and track existing, unanticipated, and emergent AI risks based on factors such as intended and actual performance in deployed contexts.
    - Compare end user and community feedback on deployed AI systems with internal performance metrics.
    - Evaluate how well metrics identify and measure new risks as they emerge.
    - Track error response times and monitor response quality.

- **Measure 3.2**: Risk-tracking approaches are considered for settings where AI risks are difficult to assess using currently available measurement techniques or where metrics are not yet available.
    - Set up processes to monitor emerging risks that can't be measured with current methods. Identify AI actors who will track these risks and create an inventory of methods.
- **Measure 3.3**: Feedback processes for end users and impacted communities to report problems and appeal system outcomes are established and integrated into AI system evaluation metrics.
    - Assess the effectiveness of processes for reporting errors by end users and operators.
    - Break down and examine the types and frequency of end user appeal requests, along with their outcomes.
    - Track participation rates and awareness of the availability of feedback activities.
- **Measure 4.0**: Feedback mechanisms are in place to measure the efficacy of measurements and metrics.
- **Measure 4.1**: Measurement approaches for identifying AI risks are connected to deployment context(s) and informed through consultation with domain experts and other end users. Approaches are documented.
    - Use end user feedback to explore how specific metrics and measurement methods work in different organizational and operational settings.

  - Examine and document how system-internal measurement processes align with the feedback collected from end users.
  - Determine and implement ways to assess effectiveness and satisfaction using end user elicitation techniques, and document the results.
- **Measure 4.2**: Measurement results regarding AI system trustworthiness in deployment context(s) and across the AI life cycle are informed by input from domain experts and other relevant AI actors to validate whether the system is performing consistently as intended. Results are documented.
  - Combine feedback from end users, operators, and those affected by the Map function to assess the AI system's trustworthiness. Make sure to consider both positive and negative feedback.
  - Assess feedback alongside the AI system's trustworthiness characteristics from Measures 2.5 to 2.11.
  - Examine feedback on end user satisfaction and confidence in the AI system's performance, including whether the output is seen as valid, reliable, and explainable.
- **Measure 4.3**: Measurable performance improvements or declines based on consultations with relevant AI actors, including affected communities, and field data about context-relevant risks and trustworthiness characteristics, are identified and documented.
  - Establish baseline metrics for trustworthy characteristics.

- Define and describe the key operation values and states at the baseline level.
- Use qualitative methods to enhance and support quantitative baseline measures, working closely with impact assessment, human factors, and socio-technical AI actors.

NIST AI RMF Manage

The Manage Function of the NIST AI Risk Management Framework (AI RMF) deals with addressing identified risks and putting strategies in place to minimize harm, track performance, and continually improve AI systems. This involves creating and carrying out mitigation plans, which include reducing bias and boosting cybersecurity, to lower identified risks. The function also covers monitoring performance to keep the AI system on track with its goals, setting up procedures to handle breaches or failures, and creating feedback loops to constantly improve governance and operational processes.

- **Manage 1.0**: AI risks are risk-based, determined by assessments and other analytical data from the Map and Measure functions.
- **Manage 1.1**: A determination is made as to whether the AI system achieves its intended purpose and stated objectives and whether its development or deployment should proceed.
    - When assessing the negative risks and benefits of AI systems, consider their trustworthiness characteristics. Use the TEVV outputs from the map and measure functions to inform risk treatment decisions. Continuously track and monitor negative risks and benefits throughout the AI system's life cycle, including after deployment monitoring.

- **Manage 1.2**: Treatment of documented AI risks is prioritized based on impact, likelihood, or available resources or methods.
  - Allocate risk management resources based on established risk tolerance levels. AI systems with lower risk tolerance receive more extensive oversight, mitigation, and management resources.
  - Record the practices and decisions used to determine AI risk tolerance and allocate resources.
  - Regularly review and adjust risk tolerance levels as needed, using information from ongoing AI system monitoring and assessment.
- **Manage 1.3**: Responses to the AI risks deemed high priority as identified by the Map function are developed, planned, and documented. Risk response options can include mitigating, transferring, avoiding, or accepting.
  - Comply with regulatory and organizational standards, as well as industry, discipline, or professional requirements, when applying risk tolerances within the organization.
  - Develop procedures for addressing AI system risks related to trustworthiness characteristics.
  - Give priority to risks that affect physical safety, legal liability, regulatory compliance, and harm to individuals, groups, or communities.
- **Manage 1.4**: Negative residual risks (defined as the sum of all unmitigated risks) to both downstream acquirers of AI systems and end users are documented.

- Record any remaining risks within risk response plans, noting those that have been accepted, transferred, or mitigated.

- **Manage 2.0**: Strategies for maximizing the AI benefits and lowering the negative impacts are planned, tested, implemented, and documented.

- **Manage 2.1**: Resources required to manage AI risks are taken into account, along with viable non-AI alternative systems, approaches, or methods, to reduce the magnitude or likelihood of potential impacts.

    - Record any remaining risks within risk response plans, noting those that have been accepted, transferred, or mitigated.

- **Manage 2.2**: Mechanisms are in place and applied to sustain the value of deployed AI systems.

    - Set up risk controls that consider trustworthiness characteristics, including: Data management, quality, and privacy controls, such as minimizing, correcting, or deleting data, as part of the organization's data governance policies. Machine learning and endpoint security measures, like robust models, differential privacy, authentication, and throttling. Business rules that adjust, limit, or restrict AI system outputs in specific situations. Using domain expertise related to the deployment context for ongoing improvement and testing across the AI life cycle. Developing and regularly tracking configurations for human-AI teaming. Protocols for assessing models and evaluating, validating, and verifying (TEVV) their performance. Using standardized documentation and transparent mechanisms. Software quality assurance practices throughout the AI life cycle. Methods to explore system limitations and avoid past failed designs or deployments.

- **Manage 2.3**: Procedures are followed to respond to and recover from a previously unknown risk when it is identified.
  - Protocols, resources, and metrics are in place to continuously monitor the performance, trustworthiness, and alignment of AI systems with contextual norms and values.
  - Set up and regularly review plans for addressing incidents, negative impacts, or outcomes.
  - Develop and maintain procedures to regularly check system components for drift, decontextualization, or other factors that impact AI system behavior.
- **Manage 2.4**: Mechanisms are in place and applied, responsibilities are assigned and understood to supersede, disengage, or deactivate AI systems that demonstrate performance or outcomes inconsistent with intended use.
  - Regularly review our existing procedures for handling AI system bypass actions. This includes plans for backup or redundant systems to ensure our operations and business continue to run smoothly. We should also regularly review the thresholds for activating or deactivating bypass

responses. To understand the potential impact of bypassing or deactivating an AI system, we should apply change management processes to identify the upstream and downstream effects components.

- **Manage 3.0**: AI risks and benefits from third parties are managed.
- **Manage 3.1**: AI risks and benefits from third-party resources are regularly monitored, and risk controls are applied and documented.
    - Use the organization's risk tolerance when dealing with third-party AI systems.
    - Develop and document plans for managing risk when it comes to third-party AI technology, personnel, or other resources.
    - Keep records and documentation up-to-date for third-party AI systems and components.
- **Manage 3.2**: Pre-trained models, which are used for development, are monitored as part of the AI system's regular monitoring and maintenance.
    - Pinpoint pre-trained models within the AI system inventory for risk-tracking purposes. Set up processes to regularly and independently evaluate the performance and trustworthiness of these pre-trained models, both on their own and as part of third-party risk monitoring. Also, keep an eye on the performance and trustworthiness of AI system components linked to pre-trained models, as part of the overall third-party risk tracking.

- **Manage 4.0**: The treatment of risks includes response and recovery, and a communication plan for the identified and measured AI risks.
- **Manage 4.1**: Post-deployment AI system monitoring plans are implemented, including mechanisms for capturing and evaluating input from users and other relevant AI actors, appeal and override, decommissioning, incident response, recovery, and change management.
    - Set up and regularly review procedures to track AI system performance for potential risks and the positive and negative effects related to trustworthiness characteristics.
    - Carry out post-deployment testing to assess the validity and reliability of the AI system, as well as its bias, fairness, privacy, security, and resilience.
    - Assess the trustworthiness of the AI system in real-world scenarios similar to its intended use, and before it's deployed.
- **Manage 4.2**: Measurable activities for continual improvements are integrated into AI system updates and include regular engagement with interested parties, including relevant AI actors.
    - Build trustworthiness into protocols and metrics that drive ongoing improvement. Create processes to gather and incorporate feedback into updates to AI systems. Evaluate and assess how proposed improvements align with relevant regulations and laws frameworks.

- Manage 4.3: Incidents and errors are communicated to relevant AI actors, including affected communities. Processes for tracking, responding to, and recovering from incidents and errors are followed and documented.
- Set up procedures to regularly share information about errors, incidents, and negative impacts with the right stakeholders, operators, practitioners, users, and those affected.
- Keep a database of reported errors, near-misses, incidents, and negative impacts, including the date reported, number of reports, impact, and severity assessment and responses.
- Also, maintain a database of system changes, the reason for the change, and details on how it was made, tested, implemented, and deployed.

ISO 42001

ISO 42001 marks a significant milestone as the inaugural international standard for Artificial Intelligence Management Systems (AIMS). It offers a helpful framework for organizations striving to build, implement, and nurture responsible AI systems across their entire life cycle. This standard thoughtfully guides AI governance and risk management, tackling important ethical issues such as bias, privacy, and accountability. By following these guidelines, organizations can promote the trustworthy and safe development and use of AI-driven products and services, fostering confidence and integrity in their AI initiatives.

The purpose of the framework is to provide organizations a systemic approach to AI risks with an emphasis on ethics, transparency, and effective deployment. The AIMS framework details requirements for AI Management Systems to include governance, AI risks, and implementing controls for AI development and operations. Core principles of the framework are about well-being, safety, privacy, fairness, accountability, and trustworthiness of the AI.

Cloud Security Alliance AI Controls Matrix (AICM)

The AI Controls Matrix (AICM) is a unique, vendor-neutral framework for cloud-based AI systems. Organizations can utilize the AICM to develop, implement, and operate AI systems in a secure and responsible way.[1] Created by industry experts, the AICM expands on CSA's Cloud Control Matrix and includes the latest AI security best practices. It features 243 control objectives distributed across 18 security domains. The AICM aligns with leading standards, such as ISO 42001, ISO 27001, NIST AI RMF 1.0, and BSI AIC4. The AICM is available for free download.

The document is thoroughly researched and documented. The AI Controls Matrix (or AICM for short) is designed to help organizations securely develop, implement, and use AI technologies. It's built on the CCM but expands it to address AI-specific risks. The first revision will include 242 controls across 18 security domains, covering everything from model security to governance and compliance. The AICM complements frameworks like NIST AI RMF, ISO/IEC 42001:2023, and the EU AI Act, offering specific and actionable guidance for organizations, as well as concrete steps for implementation and auditing. The AICM focuses on key AI security controls for model scanning, adversarial attack analysis, model poisoning mitigation, data poisoning prevention and detection, identity and access management, and more.

[1] `https://cloudsecurityalliance.org/artifacts/ai-controls-matrix`

EU AI Act[2]

The European Union's AI Act can be leveraged as a framework. Key features are it takes a risk-based approach and categorizes AI systems into four risk levels:

- Unacceptable
- High
- Limited
- Minimal Risk

There is a prohibition on some AI practices that are deemed to pose a level of risk that is unacceptable. AI systems that are deemed high risk have strict requirements that focus on human oversight, transparency, risk management, and governance. There is also the creation of a European AI Board to assist with the adoption, standards development, and promulgation.

FAIR-AIR

The FAIR Artificial Intelligence (AI) Cyber Risk Playbook is another framework that can be leveraged for AI risk management.[3] The focus in this document is intended to help identify AI loss exposure risks and enable risk-based decisions. It does this by using the FAIR techniques of quantitative analysis of risk, modeling, and quantifying cyber risk. The playbook breaks it down into five steps:

---

[2] https://www.europarl.europa.eu/topics/en/article/20230601STO93804/eu-ai-act-first-regulation-on-artificial-intelligence

[3] https://www.fairinstitute.org/blog/fair-artificial-intelligence-ai-cyber-risk-playbook

1. **Contextualize**: The start of the process is to identify and recognize the five vectors of Generative AI risk: Shadow GenAI, Creating Your Own Foundational LLM, Hosting on LLMs, Managed LLMs, and Active Cyber Attack.

2. **Identify Risk Scenarios**: This is almost a process of threat modeling, where your team thinks through possible loss exposure scenarios using their threats/ assets/effects of Factor Analysis of Information Risk (FAIR).

3. Quantify Scenarios with FAIR: Using the data, apply the FAIR analysis to produce some quantification of the risk. The example FAIR uses

    a. "There is a 5% probability in the next year that Employees will leak company-sensitive information via an open-source LLM Model (like ChatGPT), which will lead to $5 million of losses."[4]

4. **Prioritize and Treat AI Risks**: Prioritize the risks using the key drivers behind the risk scenarios.

5. **Decision Making**: Comparing risk-management options, looking at the quantitative analysis and amounts, available mitigating or compensating controls, and others to make a decision.

The framework's intent is summed up by the conclusion "*The purpose of this approach is to meet the business needs, not create additional obstacles to AI deployment.*"[5]

[4] https://www.fairinstitute.org/blog/fair-artificial-intelligence-ai-cyber-risk-playbook

[5] https://www.fairinstitute.org/blog/fair-artificial-intelligence-ai-cyber-risk-playbook

IEEE Ethically Aligned Design (EAD)

The Institute of Electrical and Electronics Engineers (IEEE) Ethically Aligned Design is a set of guidelines for prioritizing ethical considerations in autonomous and intelligent systems. This framework emphasizes humanity: human rights, well-being, data ownership, and agency.[6] It also addresses transparency, accountability, and awareness of misuse. Focusing on ethical use, it highlights high-level ethical principles and recommendations for their implementation. Additionally, it includes a section that considers different cultural contexts and future risks.

MITREs Sensible Regulatory Framework for AI Security

MITRE's Sensible Regulatory Framework for AI Security aims to establish guidelines and best practices to improve the security and resilience of AI systems.[7] It integrates technical, operational, and organizational elements to offer a comprehensive perspective on AI security. The framework focuses on risk identification and management, continuous assessments, and implementing security measures that evolve with emerging threats. It offers a solid foundation for teams aiming to secure their AI systems.

MITREs ATLAS Matrix

The Adversarial Threat Landscape for Artificial Intelligence Systems (ATLAS) Matrix provides a comprehensive overview of potential threats

[6] https://standards.ieee.org/wp-content/uploads/import/documents/other/ead_v2.pdf

[7] https://www.mitre.org/news-insights/publication/sensible-regulatory-framework-ai-security

to AI systems.[8] This framework provides a comprehensive analysis of malicious actor tactics and classifies threats across various business sectors, including finance, healthcare, and more. It offers guidance on effective countermeasures and defense strategies against attacks. For anyone seeking to understand adversarial AI risks and manage them effectively, this is the preferred framework.

Google's Secure AI Framework (SAIF)

The Google SAIF provides guidelines and tools to improve the security of AI systems throughout their life cycle.[9] Considering Google's own AI efforts, their framework incorporates security into the AI development process, including thorough threat modeling. Their use of automated testing tools can be difficult for smaller development teams, but it remains the most effective way to conduct analysis. As is typical with Google, there is a strong focus on transparency and accountability throughout the process. This framework is very proactive, emphasizing security and continuous monitoring to mitigate risks associated with AI systems.

ISO 31000

ISO 31000 isn't a specific AI framework, but its guidance is highly relevant to managing AI security risks. As an international standard for risk management, ISO 31000 outlines principles, a framework, and a process for handling risks that organizations face.[10] The standard encourages a systematic and transparent method for assessing and mitigating risks, applicable to organizations of any size or sector. Its aim is to embed risk management within an organization's governance, strategy, and planning,

[8] https://atlas.mitre.org

[9] https://safety.google/intl/en_in/safety/saif/

[10] https://www.iso.org/standards/popular/iso-31000-family

thereby increasing the likelihood of reaching goals, enhancing safety, and safeguarding assets. While ISO 31000 isn't tailored specifically for AI, its principles are highly applicable for handling AI security risks, offering a structured way to identify, analyze, and address AI-related threats.

We've gone over the main frameworks available at the time of writing, and there will surely be more developed and published in the future, along with updates to the ones we've already discussed. It's not usually about which framework is chosen, but more about selecting one and sticking with it as a guide for managing AI risks. When you look at a vendor's framework, it's not just about the choice they've made but how effectively they're following it. Whether it's NIST AI RMF or EAD, the key is to see how well the vendor's AI team and organization are reviewing each control listed in the framework, understanding the risks, and managing them effectively.

Company or Sector-Specific Frameworks

Company-specific AI governance frameworks are thoughtfully tailored applications of industry standards, such as the NIST AI Risk Management Framework or OECD Principles. These frameworks weave important AI values like fairness, transparency, and security into a company's unique way of working and its risk preferences. For example, a fintech might put explainability protocols in place for credit scoring, a healthcare provider could evaluate diagnostic AI for bias, and a global enterprise might work to detect and manage unauthorized AI tools. These adaptable frameworks are designed to meet industry-specific regulations, like HIPAA in healthcare, and align with business goals, often by involving stakeholder feedback to develop policies that truly fit their needs.

How to Make Your Own AI Framework

If none of the existing frameworks are to your liking or strategic goals, then there is nothing wrong with creating your own. This is usually accomplished by adapting principles from multiple, reputable standards like NIST AI Risk Management Framework (AI RMF), including govern, map, measure, and manage functions. Align your AI risk management framework with your governance structure and corporate strategy. Incorporate into your framework industry-specific requirements to ensure your policies and processes fit your challenges. Governance requires firm establishment of roles and ownership; for example, determine and document who leads AI development, data management, compliance, and other key roles. Utilize AI governance tools that exist for scanning of features like bias, transparency, and performance tracking.

Examples of Industry-Specific Implementation of Frameworks

Financial Services: A fintech company adopts a framework to make sure its credit scoring AI systems are fair, transparent, and in line with ethical standards. They do this by implementing explainability protocols for each decision, helping everyone feel more confident and trust in the process.

Healthcare: A healthcare provider implements a framework to verify the accuracy and safety of diagnostic AI models, including regular risk evaluations and quarterly compliance reviews to adhere to patient data protection and privacy regulations.

Manufacturing: Companies develop frameworks for predictive maintenance systems, leveraging AI compliance models to prevent equipment failures and ensure worker safety.

Retail: Companies implement governance models for their recommendation algorithms to make sure they respect privacy standards and avoid bias, which helps build trust with consumers.

Global Enterprises: A large enterprise implements a framework with AI asset discovery to monitor and control the use of unapproved generative AI tools by employees, reducing security and compliance risks.

Challenges with AI RMF Framework Implementation

As with anything we do in business, there will be challenges. There are a few categories of issues most organizations will encounter with the adoption of any AI Risk Management Framework (RMF). Leverage this information to determine how well your vendors are leveraging their AI RMF.

Organizational Issues

Implementing an AI risk management framework frequently necessitates substantial organizational change, which may encounter resistance. Many entities face difficulties in integrating AI risk management activities into their existing frameworks and processes, particularly if they lack a culture of responsible innovation or extensive experience with AI technologies. Facilitating collaboration among diverse teams can also present challenges. AI development often occurs within specialized units, and uniting technical experts with stakeholders such as legal, ethics, and business divisions can be difficult. Siloed structures may develop, resulting in a fragmented understanding of AI risks and inconsistent management practices. Effective AI risk management demands considerable investments of time, personnel, and financial resources, which can be challenging to justify, especially given that the benefits of risk management are frequently intangible or realization may be delayed.

Technical Challenges

One of the main challenges in putting an AI risk management framework into place is how quickly AI technologies are changing and how complex they are. As AI systems grow more advanced, their decision-making can become less clear and harder to understand. This lack of transparency makes it more difficult to assess and manage potential risks effectively.

Figure 2-7. *Challenges with AI RMF Implementation*

Additionally, the rapid speed and large scale of AI systems make it tricky to spot and handle risks in a timely manner. AI models can analyze huge amounts of data and make decisions much faster than humans, which means risks can grow quickly before anyone notices or steps in to help.

Another technical challenge involves thoroughly testing AI systems. Unlike traditional software, AI models, especially those based on machine learning, can sometimes act unexpectedly in new situations not covered in their training datasets. Because AI responses can be unpredictable, it becomes more challenging to ensure they work reliably in all possible scenarios.

Furthermore, the interconnected nature of AI systems with other technological components and data sources adds additional complexity to risk management. Alterations in data patterns, changes in user behavior, or updates to interconnected systems can all influence an AI system's performance and risk profile, necessitating more real-time continuous monitoring and flexible strategies.

Regulatory Issues

The regulatory landscape for AI is quite dynamic and ever-changing, which can make it tricky to decide on the best risk management framework to follow. Different regions often have their own requirements for AI systems, and sometimes these rules can even clash, posing compliance challenges for global organizations. As technology advances quickly, it often outpaces regulatory updates, leading to periods of uncertainty where organizations need to make risk-related decisions without clear guidance. This situation can either slow down innovation or, on the other hand, encourage risky practices that might not comply once new rules are introduced.

Additionally, understanding and applying regulations to specific AI use cases can be tough, especially since many current rules weren't originally made with AI in mind. This leaves organizations to interpret these regulations themselves, which can sometimes lead to legal risks if they misjudge how to comply.

Ethical Risks

Implementing AI risk management frameworks can be quite challenging, especially when it comes to navigating the ethical dilemmas they often reveal. AI systems have the power to make decisions that deeply affect individuals and society, which brings up important questions about fairness, accountability, and human values.

A common ethical hurdle is finding the right balance between the potential benefits of AI and its possible risks. Deciding how to prioritize these concerns can be tricky without clear-cut answers.

Since AI development and use happen across the globe, cultural differences also pose ethical challenges. What one culture considers ethical in AI use might be seen differently elsewhere, making it more complex to create universally accepted risk management practices.

Another important issue is transparency and explainability. While these are widely recognized as key principles in AI ethics, organizations often face tough choices when full transparency could mean exposing personal privacy or proprietary information. Striking a balance between these competing needs requires thoughtfulness and careful decision-making.

Although AI risk management frameworks offer helpful guidance, putting them into practice isn't always easy. Success depends on having a comprehensive approach coupled with a dedicated commitment to continuous learning, adaptation, and ethical reflection.

AI by TPRM Phase

There are some methods specific to each phase in TPRM that can guide how assessments of AI in vendor networks are performed. How the team approaches assessments in each of the phases will vary on the relationship with the vendor and how risky the vendor is to the organization.

Governance and Oversight

This phase is where the groundwork is laid for proper governance and oversight of the TPRM program. The updates to this phase for AI risks are about ensuring that all program and process documentation is updated to include the identification, assessment, and management of AI risks. Some of the changes required will vary by program size, regulatory burden, complexity, and more factors, but the primary drivers will be how you currently identify, assess, and manage risks (particularly cybersecurity risks) for your third parties.

There are a couple of changes a team can make to their existing governance program (or add a new program if needed) that will address AI risks in your third parties. First, ensure that any changes you've identified in each of the subsequent phases, such as changes to the Inherent Risk Assessment (IRA), any additional questions added to due diligence questionnaires, additional policy updates or documentation that might be requested related to AI risks, updates to continuous monitoring activities, and requirements for disengagement are documented, communicated to key stakeholders, and inform training updates. After making changes to your program and policy documentation, it is a good idea to do some "test runs" with production data to validate that the changes are effective and accomplish the AI risk identification, assessment, and management goals set out in your overall TPRM program.

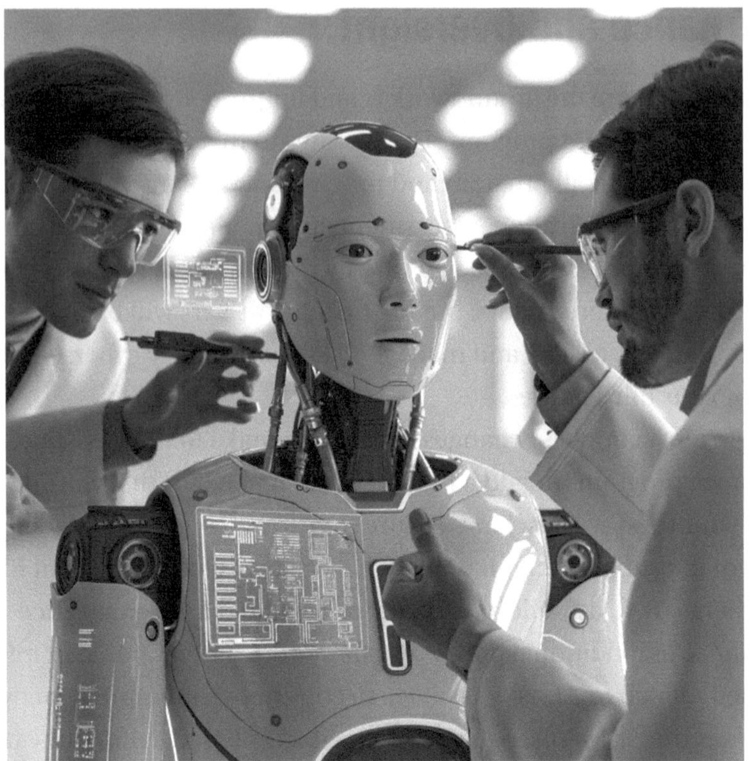

Figure 2-8. *Assess the Vendor for AI Risks*

Pre-Contract Due Diligence

Recall that the pre-contract phase is the most important for the vendor life cycle because it is when the vendor is the most attentive to our needs as a customer. The contract is not yet signed, and so vendors are more willing to answer your questions and make changes to items to get the contract signed.

One of the first things to complete in this phase is the Inherent Risk Assessment (IRA), where the initial discovery of what risk domains are relevant to this vendor is made. This phase includes risk impact identification. Adding a single question to your IRA of "Does this vendor use or produce AI or models?" is a good idea. It might be that your existing cybersecurity questions in the IRA are sufficient to cover AI risk, but because of the uniqueness of some of the risks with AI (hallucinations, anyone?), it is wise to ask this separately.

Within the pre-contract phase, and let's assume that in the course of the IRA, the business has replied "Yes" to the use of AI or a model for the third party. Now that the trigger has been set for this risk domain (AI), there needs to be an AI assessment by whoever in your governance structure is the owner of the risk evaluation process. Once the owner and/or team have gotten the vendor details as part of the TPRM process, then the decision on how much due diligence and due care the vendor receives should be risk-based. Let's break it down by risk category of High, Medium, and Low. If you are using quantitative analysis or have more than three qualitative levels, then adjust the categories in risk-based order. All work at this point is done based on the vendor's inherent risk level. After the evaluation of controls, we can determine residual risk.

Low-Risk AI Due Diligence

These vendors are low risk, and the effort to assess them should match their risk level: low. The mantra of a "risk-based approach" exists because no organization has unlimited resources or time, and categorizing vendors by risk levels allows leadership to allocate resources more effectively. For vendors with low inherent risk that also select "yes" to an AI risk question, taking the recommended risk-based approach, this category of vendors could be skipped for assessment. However, if your organization's program calls for some due diligence and due care in this category, keep it minimal.

Low-Risk Vendor AI Intake Due Diligence

- **Encryption**: Request to verify they encrypt at rest, in motion, and in process to ensure the data is kept secret. Encryption is a bare-minimum requirement for all systems with sensitive data. Ensuring that your low-risk vendors have completed this basic task is best practice.

- **AI Policy**: Ensure they have an AI policy that governs their development, testing, and updates to their AI systems. Governance is a key element in securing any system, particularly an AI system that has so many complexities.
- **Logging and Monitoring**: Request that they validate that logging and monitoring are done for all activity in their enterprise. Logging and monitoring are how anomalous behavior is detected. If there is a breach, it is also how forensics is performed to determine the root cause and fix it.
- **Robust Access Controls**: Access controls for the vendor should be above bare minimums, especially around access to the AI systems. Request that they verify their Identity and Access Management (IAM) and Privileged Access Management (PAM) are well-governed and managed.

As a low-risk vendor, these four items are sufficient to identify risk. If they answer any of the questions in the negative, assess the amount of risk due to a negative response, and then manage that identified risk. How far your teams go to validate these items is determined by your ability to engage and process the data. If your team is small, then it could be a simple yes or no question that asks the vendor to validate. If the team is a bit larger and able to perform the analysis, then you could request copies of the documents and artifacts. Typically, though, this level of risk would be more of a quick check (if resources are available). If the vendor responded in the affirmative that controls are in place and operating effectively, then no further action is required.

Medium-Risk Vendor AI Intake Due Diligence

A medium-risk vendor, as logic would dictate, will receive a bit more due diligence than a low-risk vendor, but not as much as the high-risk vendor. In terms of due diligence questions, it would be reasonable to ask what is included in the above low-risk vendor AI intake due diligence questions, with a small addition:

- **Secure Design Life Cycle (SDLC)**: Obtain some level of assurance that the vendor has a process to ensure security is part of the development process.

High-Risk Vendor AI Intake Due Diligence

This category, by definition, is going to get the most attention in the process. Vendors in this category should be receiving a list of questions that will identify and validate AI-related controls. Many of the questions should be driven by what framework your organization is using, for enterprise risk management or specifically, AI risk management. For the purpose of this book, we will utilize the NIST AI RMF to provide best-practice questions for AI due diligence on intake:

- High Risk Vendor AI Questionnaire (NIST AI RMF)[11]
    - *What framework are you using to manage AI risk?*
    - *Do you have policies, procedures, and practices in place to determine the needed level of risk management for AI?*
    - *Are the characteristics of trustworthy AI integrated into organizational policies, processes, procedures, and practices?*

[11] https://www.nist.gov/itl/ai-risk-management-framework

- *Are the legal and regulatory requirements involving AI understood, managed, and documented?*
- *Are there mechanisms in place to inventory AI systems and are they resourced according to organizational risk priorities?*
- *Are there processes and procedures in place for decommissioning and phasing out AI systems safely and in a manner that does not increase risks or decrease the organization's trustworthiness?*
- *Are the Roles, responsibilities, and lines of communication related to mapping, measuring, and managing AI risks documented and clear to individuals and teams throughout the organization?*
- *Does the Executive leadership of the organization take responsibility for decisions about risks associated with AI system development and deployment?*
- *Are organizational policies and practices in place to foster a critical thinking and safety-first mindset in the design, development, deployment, and use of AI systems to minimize potential negative impacts?*
- *Are organizational policies and practices in place to collect, consider, prioritize, and integrate feedback from those external to the team that developed or deployed the AI system regarding the potential individual and societal impacts related to AI risks?*
- *Are there Policies and procedures in place that address AI risks associated with third-party entities, including risks of infringement of a third party's intellectual property or other rights?*

- *Are the organization's mission and relevant goals for AI technology understood and documented?*
- *Has the business value or context of business use been clearly defined or, in the case of assessing existing AI systems, re-evaluated?*
- *Confirm System requirements (e.g., "the system shall respect the privacy of its users") are elicited from and understood by relevant AI actors. Design decisions take into account the socio-technical implications to address AI risks.*
- *Are the specific tasks and methods used to implement the tasks that the AI system will support are defined (e.g., classifiers, generative models, recommenders).*
- *Is the information about the AI system's knowledge limits and how the system output may be utilized and overseen by humans documented? Documentation provides sufficient information to assist relevant AI actors when making decisions and taking subsequent actions.*
- *Are the potential benefits of intended AI system functionality and performance examined and documented?*
- *The potential costs, including non-monetary costs resulting from expected or realized AI errors or system functionality and trustworthiness, as related to organizational risk tolerance, are examined and documented.*

- *Is the targeted application scope specified and documented based on the system's capability, established context, and AI system categorization?*
- *Is the Likelihood and magnitude of each identified impact (both potentially beneficial and harmful) based on expected use, past uses of AI systems in similar contexts, public incident reports, feedback from those external to the team that developed or deployed the AI system, or other data identified and documented?*
- *Are the practices and personnel for supporting regular engagement with relevant AI actors and integrating feedback about positive, negative, and unanticipated impacts in place and documented?*
- *Is a determination made as to whether the AI system achieves its intended purposes and stated objectives, and whether its development or deployment should proceed?*
- *Is the handling of documented AI risks prioritized based on impact, likelihood, and available resources or methods?*
- *Responses to the AI risks deemed high priority, as identified by the map function, are developed, planned, and documented. Risk response options can include mitigating, transferring, avoiding, or accepting.*
- *Are negative residual risks (defined as the sum of all unmitigated risks) to both downstream acquirers of AI systems and end users documented?*

- *Are resources required to manage AI risks taken into account, along with viable non-AI alternative systems, approaches, or methods, to reduce the magnitude or likelihood of potential impacts?*
- *Are mechanisms in place and applied to sustain the value of deployed AI systems?*
- *Are Procedures followed to respond to and recover from a previously unknown risk when it is identified?*
- *Are mechanisms in place and applied, and responsibilities are assigned and understood, to supersede, disengage, or deactivate AI systems that demonstrate performance or outcomes inconsistent with intended use.*
- *Are AI risks and benefits from third-party resources regularly monitored, and risk controls are applied and documented?*
- *Pre-trained models, which are used for development, are monitored as part of the AI system's regular monitoring and maintenance.*
- *Are post-deployment AI system monitoring plans implemented, including mechanisms for capturing and evaluating input from users and other relevant AI actors, appeal and override, decommissioning, incident response, recovery, and change management?*
- *Measurable activities for continual improvements are integrated into AI system updates and include regular engagement with interested parties, including relevant AI actors.*

- *Incidents and errors are communicated to relevant AI actors, including affected communities. Processes for tracking, responding to, and recovering from incidents and errors are followed and documented.*

Consider this a list that can be used à la carte or in full, meaning do not feel obligated to use all the questions or controls on the list. Find the ones that matter to your organization. You may also find other questions from other frameworks and incorporate them as well.

Critical Risk Vendor AI Intake Due Diligence

This category of vendor requires a special definition and isn't something that should be a typical vendor going through the process. Critical vendors are those that are so important to your own business operations that if they fail to operate, it will impact your ability to operate. Every business has these vendors that they rely on to be able to perform their day-to-day operations. The number of vendors in this category is small. There is no set number, but it should be approaching a tiny top of 1% to 10% of your vendor pool (depending on your organization's size). For these vendors, because the relationship is so crucial, there will be important steps and questions throughout the life cycle.

If a vendor is identified as critical during intake or classified as critical subsequently, there should be an additional level of scrutiny for AI risks. Aside from what has already been discussed above for the lower levels of risk, the additional work would be physical validation of the vendor programs. This can be a challenge during intake to schedule, but it is the best way to identify risks, assess them, and then manage them in cooperation with the vendor. We will lay out what to do in a physical validation exercise for an AI vendor under the Continuous Monitoring section below. Leverage that guidance to perform a physical validation, even a virtual one with collaboration tools, to get a true understanding of the risk and security at the third party.

If a physical validation is not possible, then perform as thorough a High-Risk AI evaluation as available and schedule a physical validation for a later time but as soon as possible. If your program is not mature enough or budget and resources make a physical validation impossible, then the recommendation is to do a similar validation but through virtual means.

Contract Review

During the contract phase, there are some best practices to consider when it comes to adding AI risk considerations from a vendor. While some of these are not exclusive to AI risk and are just good general practices, like including a section on incident notification, there are also specific AI contract clauses to think about. These include addressing who owns the intellectual property (IP) of the AI and the content it generates, clarifying data usage and privacy rights for training and other purposes, and providing clear definitions of the AI's role and how it can be used. It's also important to include strong security and liability clauses to help manage risks, as well as provisions for transparency and auditability to promote accountability. Additionally, parties should agree on who owns the prompts used by AI, set performance standards and risk management strategies, and stay prepared for new and upcoming AI regulations. There are a few buckets these clauses can be put into:

Transparency and Accountability

Ensure the contract has language that the vendor maintains audit trails and provides transparency mechanisms to show how the AI operates and makes decisions. Ensure the transparency of the AI's limitations and have mechanisms that address accountability if the model is not working as expected.

Security and Liability

The contract must address how the vendor implements measures to protect the AI and other data from cyberattacks and unauthorized access. Address potential risks and allocate liability for biases, errors, or bad outcomes as a result of the AI. Lastly, ensure there are provisions for risk management frameworks and plans to address any potential AI-related risks or issues.

AI Role and Scope

Any agreement should contain language to define the specific uses for the AI system and very specific statements about what is restricted from being done or performed. Clearly separate the responsibilities for the AI system and the human personnel who are engaged with the process.

Data Use and Privacy

Contracts should contain clauses to detail how sensitive data can be used for AI training, modification, or other reasons. Data retention and deletion obligations should be established for securely storing and deleting data after the contract. Lastly, the confidentiality clauses should ensure there are robust measures to protect sensitive information from unauthorized access or use by the AI.

Intellectual Property

Clearly define the ownership of the AI system and any data used to train it, along with any content or work product generated by the AI. Specify who owns the input prompts provided to the AI and any content created by it.

Others

Other areas to focus on are Performance and Service levels, to set clear performance goals and metrics for the AI system. Compliance language to include clauses requiring adherence to current and future AI laws and standards. Ensure there is an incident notification clause for any event, incident, or breach. There should be language on Change Control related to the vendor having a process established to manage changes in the AI system. Lastly, a Force Majeure clause to protect both parties from liability for unforeseen events that prevent business from proceeding.

Continuous Monitoring

The Continuous monitoring phase is where the vendor has been fully onboarded, contracts signed, and they are in production. The identification of risk does not stop, but must continue for the life of the vendor until Disengagement. There are three distinct activities during this phase that are relevant to AI risk: Cyber Continuous Monitoring, Due Diligence Questionnaires, and Physical Validations.

Cyber Continuous Monitoring

Cyber Continuous Monitoring is a program that entails using whatever tools are available at your enterprise to identify, assess, and manage vendor risk on an ongoing basis. Typically, these involve vendor risk rating software and other intelligence software to monitor vendors in near real time. One similarity the majority of these tools have is to provide a score or rating for what their algorithm gauges as a vendor risk or risks. They are typically in a grade form of A to F or a score form of 0 to 100, which provides the user with an overall temperature of the vendor risk environment. For the purposes of cybersecurity and AI, it is suggested to ignore the score itself. These scores have a lot of considerations in them that you have no way to change or fully understand. Instead, concentrate on what the specific threats, alerts, and vulnerabilities are, and focus on those. For example, these tools will alert you to botnet infections, open ports, bad DNS configurations, etc., that are real risks. Look to see if the software your team is currently using offers any alerts that are relevant to AI risk. If you are unsure, many of the software manufacturers will provide customer success teams you can query or online FAQs that are great sources to discover what actual risks are identified in their tools.

Another way to perform this monitoring is to leverage current tools in your enterprise. For example, many medium-to-larger companies will have threat intelligence teams and network security teams. It would be wise to ask the threat intelligence team if they see any negative or risk-related intel about your "critical" vendors, to alert your team. Alerting the network security team to look for any PII going to or coming from a certain vendor across the network, unencrypted, is another way to leverage your partners in the enterprise.

***Figure 2-9.** Cyber Continuous Monitoring*

Next, be sure to tie the risk identified within the tool or tools to the vendor's residual risk rating. If the alert comes through for a low-risk vendor, the risk-based approach still applies. Unless the vendor risk level is mis-assessed or has changed, then it is unlikely the alert is going to require action. However, if the vendor is a higher-risk vendor, action will be taken. Where that line is for when your team engages or does not engage the third party in conversation regarding risk identified is called a risk tolerance level, and it needs to be determined by your enterprise risk management team or company.

Due Diligence Questionnaires

Most organizations still send out questionnaires to vendors once a year or more often, depending upon risk level. For those vendors where the risk is higher and a physical validation is not warranted or required, then a questionnaire is an acceptable way to assess vendor AI risk, if you are also obtaining evidence to validate the controls your organization deems critical. However, it should be tailored to only the questions that are important to your team to identify and assess risk. Asking hundreds upon hundreds of questions is not the goal. The goal is to ask about what you care about.

Regarding an AI due diligence questionnaire, it can follow similar steps described in the intake due diligence section by risk level. Low-risk vendors will be a very slim question set, if any at all. Medium risk vendors will get some variation of the low-risk questionnaire and the high-risk question sets. High-risk vendors will get as many questions as your team deems necessary to identify and assess AI risk at this top level of vendor risk. Lastly, critical vendors will get a physical validation (next sub-section) to ensure they are doing their best at AI security. One last thing about this phase is with regard to the cadence and frequency of re-reviews that occur. Whether you send these questionnaires out every year, every other year, or at other frequencies, ensure your logic is spelled out in your governance documentation and is followed.

Physical Validation

A physical validation is the gold standard of risk identification and assessment. These exercises involve teammates going to the vendor site or sites and physically checking that the security is in place as described by the vendor. A good analogy used in the past: The difference between a remote questionnaire and a physical validation is the difference between asking your kids if their room is clean and you, as the parent, going to check the cleanliness of the room. It isn't that your vendor is lying or not being as transparent as they could, but it is the difference in witnessing the actions or evidence of them that makes a difference.

In a risk-based approach, physical validation will only be done on those vendors where the risk threshold in your organization describes the level of vendor risk required for this exercise to be completed. Because this takes a little bit more effort than simply sending a remote questionnaire, the vendors that are chosen for a physical validation should be described thoroughly in your governance documentation.

A physical validation can be done in two different ways. On-site, where your team goes to the vendor location(s) to perform the physical validation. These are best done when a vendor has their own data center or uses a co-location facility, or when the vendor sits at the top of your risk pile and warrants that level of attention. A virtual physical validation requires minimal travel because you leverage collaboration tools like Zoom and Teams to connect with the vendor's SMEs and validate policy and process. These are best done with vendors who have data at a Cloud Service Provider (CSP) because you will not be able to tour the cloud facility at a CSP. A virtual physical validation also allows for more flexibility for scheduling with the vendor.

For a physical validation performed for a vendor with AI, do not take the remote questionnaires and ask them in person. That is not a great use of your time. Use this opportunity to have a conversation with the vendor about their security, not simply asking yes or no questions. Using the NIST AI RMF as guidance, we can demonstrate how controls can be turned into a conversational question for the vendor.

Taking the Govern category, specifically the Govern 1.0 category, the controls are as such:

- **Govern 1.1**: Legal and regulatory requirements involving AI are understood, managed, and documented.

- **Govern 1.2**: The characteristics of trustworthy AI are integrated into organizational policies, processes, procedures, and practices.
- **Govern 1.3**: Processes, procedures, and practices are in place to determine the needed level of risk management activities based on the organization's risk tolerance.
- **Govern 1.4**: The risk management process and its outcomes are established through transparent policies, procedures, and other controls based on organizational risk priorities.
- **Govern 1.5**: Ongoing monitoring and periodic review of the risk management process and its outcomes are planned and organizational roles and responsibilities clearly defined, including determining the frequency of periodic review.
- **Govern 1.6**: Mechanisms are in place to inventory AI systems and are resourced according to organizational risk priorities.
- **Govern 1.7**: Processes and procedures are in place for decommissioning and phasing out AI systems safely and in a manner that does not increase risks or decrease the organization's trustworthiness.

To convert these into conversations, change the controls into questions that elicit transparency:

- **Govern 1.1**: How does your organization understand, manage, and document the Legal and regulatory requirements involving AI.

    - Ask them to show this in a policy or process document.

- **Govern 1.2**: How are the characteristics of trustworthy AI integrated into organizational policies, processes, procedures, and practices?
    - Demonstrate this by showing their AI policies, processes, and procedures, and then have them show how this has been done at least once in production.
- **Govern 1.3**: Discuss the processes, procedures, and practices in place to determine the needed level of risk management activities based on the organization's risk tolerance.
    - Demonstrate this by showing their AI policies, processes, and procedures, and then have them show how this has been done at least once in production.
- **Govern 1.4**: Is the risk management process and its outcomes established through transparent policies, procedures, and other controls based on organizational risk priorities.
    - Demonstrate this by showing the relevant policies, processes, and procedures, and then have them show how this has been done at least once in production.
- **Govern 1.5**: Talk about the ongoing monitoring and periodic review of the risk management process and its outcomes. Are organizational roles and responsibilities clearly defined, including determining the frequency of periodic review?

    - Demonstrate this by showing the relevant policies, processes, and procedures, and then have them show how this has been done at least once in production.

- **Govern 1.6**: Describe the mechanisms in place to inventory AI systems and resources according to organizational risk priorities.
    - Demonstrate this by showing the relevant policies, processes, and procedures, and then have them show how this has been done at least once in production

- **Govern 1.7**: Describe the processes and procedures in place for decommissioning and phasing out AI systems safely and in a manner that does not increase risks or decrease the organization's trustworthiness.
    - Demonstrate this by showing the relevant policies, processes, and procedures, and then have them show how this has been done at least once in production.

These process walkthroughs can be done for every control in the NIST AI RMF, or you can take the framework your organization uses for managing AI risk and configure it similarly. The idea here is that you're confirming the vendor has proper governance documentation and processes in place, and then validating they are following their governance by having them show proof of it happening in production. If the vendor cannot produce the governance documentation or prove they are performing as described in production, then there is a gap needs to be addressed.

Disengagement

Disengaging from a vendor is a process that a lot of TPRM programs rush through or don't do well, mostly because we don't offboard third parties very often. Businesses hang on to vendors for a long, long time, and so while we get a lot of practice onboarding third parties, we get only sporadic practice disengaging with vendors. In this phase, there are some key steps related to data security, connectivity, and some steps specific to AI.

First, best practice is to have a playbook or runbook for how disengagement is carried out. In this document, all disengagement steps and responsibilities are outlined in a standardized checklist to ensure consistency and completeness. Second, it is essential that your system of record (SoR) contains accurate and current information. The SoR for your third parties should be updated continually and accurately so that the identity of every application, service, and data source the AI interacts with is mapped correctly and can facilitate offboarding those sensitive areas. Finally, there must be a trigger to start the process; initiate the offboarding workflow when a vendor's departure is confirmed, often with integration from the TPRM and/or business owners.

Once the trigger for departure has been activated and the team has collected the offboarding checklist with complete and accurate data from the system of record, the disengagement process can begin. First, revoke all access, ideally by automating the process through deactivating all user accounts and revoking access to systems, databases, and networks to prevent unauthorized access from the vendor. Depending on how the contracts are written, determine the data owner and ensure it is either properly destroyed (with a Certificate of Destruction) or kept secure during any legal or regulatory hold. Deprovisioning of the AI application or system should be completed across all platforms (test, dev, production) and documented.

Once the vendor has been fully offboarded, the work is not quite complete. There is a monitoring period once a vendor is offboarded to ensure nothing lingers. Leverage your network and access monitoring teams at your organization to scan and alert your team if any instance of that vendor appears post disengagement. Run a scan for at least a month or a quarter to ensure there are no unknown connections or access from the vendor not in the system of record.

Continuous Improvement

This phase of TPRM is ongoing and includes all other phases necessary for improvement. Given the rapid pace of change with AI and the many unknowns, it is best practice to review your AI-related policy and program every six months instead of the typical annual review for a TPRM program. Use the framework your team has chosen to manage AI risk and assess whether any changes or updates are sufficient to warrant adjustments to your program. Review your experiences with AI vendors to identify lessons learned that need to be incorporated. Set metrics and goals to achieve implementation of the updates, making the next six-month review easier for the team. Last, ensure there are mechanisms within your organization to alert you when there are emerging AI risks and/or changes in AI regulations that need to be considered.

In conclusion to the AI risk by the TPRM phase, there are a few changes required to the program itself to account for the challenges posed by AI risk. Always start with small changes, learn from any mistakes or challenges encountered, and then expand as your comfort and resources allow.

Offshore AI Vendor Evaluations

Offshore vendors are those not within your geographic country, often used to extend customer service times and business support. To perform an offshore security assessment, first define the scope and identify assets at risk. Then assess vulnerabilities by inspecting physical security and IT systems, and evaluate threats by analyzing likelihood and impact. Based on these findings, document the risks and prioritize mitigation strategies, such as implementing new security measures or refining existing procedures. Finally, implement the recommendations and conduct regular reviews to ensure ongoing security.

For offshore AI vendors, there needs to be a decision if the vendor is enough risk to either warrant an offshore assessment by your organization or have a proxy perform it within the country of origin. You can also choose to not perform an offshore assessment. If the vendor poses enough risk, then an offshore physical validation at the vendor's facilities is recommended and considered best practice. This is best done by your own team, but if you do not have the resources to do an offshore/overseas assessment, look to a consulting firm (like one of the big four accounting firms) that has a presence in the country where the vendor is located, and have them perform it per your directions and requirements.

In terms of what and how to assess, it is very similar to a normal physical validation, except there may be additional physical security validations depending on the vendor type. For example, in many of these offshore locations, the vendor is engaging with customers and their sensitive data. This level of access to sensitive information requires an extra layer of security in areas where they are going to have this level of access. Checking to ensure they don't allow any recording devices (cell phones, cameras) into the production areas is one of those steps that isn't typical of a physical validation onshore.

There are a couple of key factors to determine in an offshore assessment:

- **Pre-planning**: Determining the risk level of an offshore vendor that will require an assessment must be driven by your governance documentation. Once you determine if you will assess an offshore vendor, then there should be an additional set of controls, given the differing risks.

- **Planning**: This is the phase where conversations are taking place with the vendor to arrange the on-site or offshore visit. Items like scope, dates, SMEs needed for discussions, and other items to review during the visit. Ensure you pay attention to when you're requesting a visit, as vacation schedules and national holidays will affect SME availability. In addition, during this phase, any pre-work for the visit can be accomplished, like visas and travel arrangements as needed.
- **On-site Visit**: During the visit, there will be a whirlwind of meetings with SMEs and leaders from both teams, more than likely. Visits from the clients (i.e., your organization) are not common for many of these groups, and they will generally treat you very well. Remember that while the hospitality is nice, the primary purpose is to assess their AI security (among other items). All your pre-planning and planning work, with the appropriate governance, will guide the team in each step. If some obvious risks or gaps result in findings, it is good to validate each issue with the third party and verbally share what is likely to make it in a report so they can get a head start on fixing them.
- Much of the difference between a normal onsite visit and an offshore visit will involve physical security validations. Check to see if they enforce checking personnel who will access production data for recording devices. Are the cameras and recordings of the work areas sufficient in coverage and duration of hold (typically 90 days). How well are they checking and validating personnel upon check-in, as well as performing personnel background checks?

- **Report and Wrap-Up**: This part of the process is usually completed once the assessors have returned to their home country and have had time to process the data. There may be some continued back-and-forth as the teams share findings and remediation plans, as well as providing evidence to validate issue closure . Ensure initial findings and remediation plans are noted in a final report. Those findings and plans should then be transferred to a central repository for issue management and follow-up. Once the vendor provides evidence a finding is closed, the evidence must be validated by the assessor to ensure it meets your organization's expectations. Continue to ensure you update the system of record with all relevant data.

Use-Case (AI SaaS Software)

One of the best ways to explain concepts and make them relatable to readers is to provide a use-case and walk through an example. We will take a fake company, developing and selling AI SaaS software (let's say it is Human Resources software that is online and offers AI capabilities to users and customers). We will call this company "OpusNox." OpusNox leverages NIST AI RMF for its AI risk management framework. The nice advantage of OpusNox is it makes available a "trust center" on its website, which provides clients with access to its SOC and ISO reports for evaluation alongside the AI. We will analyze this software by phase, imagining you work for a company considering integrating OpusNox into your organization as its new HR solution. Additionally, since there are different levels of maturity in TPRM and AI, we will offer two levels of maturity for evaluating AI risk within each phase. The focus will be on risk identification and assessment methods at each maturity level, not the actual risk level, as that will vary depending on the customer, product, use, and other factors.

Use-Case Governance and Oversight

While this isn't really confined to the OpusNox instance, this phase is important in how it will set up the subsequent steps for AI risk reviews and mitigation within the TPRM program. This involves updating and managing your governance documentation to include AI. Changes should already be made by the time a vendor comes through the system.

Less Mature Programs

Governance in these programs is typically lighter or can be more ad hoc. Look to the specific risks for identifying, assessing, and managing AI risks in your vendor relationships and update as appropriate. Perform walk-throughs of the process and programs with stakeholders and appropriate SMEs to ensure no steps for identifying and managing AI risks are missing.

More Mature Programs

More evolved programs will likely have more automated systems that will need updating to account for the updates in identifying, assessing, and managing AI risk from vendors. Ensure the changes account for the AI framework adoption and the workflows are tested before production.

Use-Case Pre-Contract

In this phase, we are performing our due diligence and due care for the vendor, assuming the business case and budget have been approved. The steps for each will not vary, but how they are accomplished may.

Less Mature Programs

If your TPRM program is very new and doesn't have an IRA form, there is a great free one available on the Third Party Risk Association's website. This questionnaire contains 15 questions that are ideal for the trigger questions expected in an inherent risk assessment, which includes the question "Is the third party leveraging AI/ML in any capacity (within their own environment or from their third party)?" If your organization already has an IRA, then leverage the one from TPRA to see how close yours is to best practice.

The question noted above should be your trigger for assessing OpusNox from an AI perspective. In fact, based on the information described in the use case overview section, the following assessments should trigger

- **Cybersecurity Risk Assessment**: With sensitive data being shared (personnel data is PII), the fact that there is likely to be a network connection needed to upload and download HR data, it would trigger this assessment.
- **Compliance Risk Assessment**: Personnel data has a number of regulatory oversight and laws governing it. This software will definitely have compliance risk associated with it.
- **Privacy Risk Assessment**: Sensitive data will be used with personnel and potential candidate information, necessitating this type of assessment.
- **Operational Risk Assessment**: Because a company cannot operate without its human component, and those components need to be paid, promoted, fired, transferred, evaluated, and more, the HR software will mitigate some of this risk.

- **AI Risk Assessment**: The team is going to be using their AI-enabled products; therefore, this assessment would be triggered.
- **Financial Risk Assessment**: This assessment would also trigger based on how expensive HR software usually is.

Since it triggered the above risk assessments, there will need to be additional due diligence work for these risk domains. For the AI risk domain, the team can leverage the third party's trust center that contains some useful artifacts. How deeply you leverage the trust portal will depend on your TPRM program maturity and the risk level of the vendor. In this case, since it is an HR software vendor that will house lots of sensitive data, a connection to your organization's network, and potentially has compliance risk, privacy risk, operational risk, and AI risk, it is a High inherent risk vendor. There is an argument to be made that the HR software vendor could be a Critical risk vendor, depending on how important staffing is to your success. In addition, OpusNox has provided the following documents to review on their trust center:

- ISO 27001 Certificate for most products
- ISO 27017 Certificate for most products
- ISO 27018 Certificate for most products
- ISO 27701 Certificate for most products
- ISO 42001 Report for most products
- NIST AI Risk Management Framework Attestation
- SIG Questionnaire
- Data Privacy Framework Certification
- TRUSTe Certification

- HIPPA Certification Attestation
- FedRAMP Medium Attestation

In a program still maturing, these attestations are typically sufficient to provide the level of detail necessary to assess the risk, identifying any gaps between the controls expected and those found in the documentation. They should be mapped to the controls you find critical to evaluate to ensure coverage. For OpusNox, there is ample documentation for most less mature programs to identify, assess, and mitigate the risk for the AI risk domain. Clicking on the link to the NIST AI RMF Attestation takes us to a letter from the assessor company that performed the risk assessment. As a risk professional, observing that they had an outside company (not themselves) perform the NIST AI RMF assessment makes the attestation much more valuable, if there are no high-risk findings noted. Focus on the Scope statement of the attestation to ensure it covers the products and areas of interest, as well as the Conclusion:

> *"CONCLUSION*
>
> *The Assessment determined that OpusNox's RAI Governance Program is well-structured and effectively supports AI risk management across the organization. The program demonstrates strong governance, clear oversight mechanisms, and a commitment to continuous improvement in alignment with NIST AI Risk Management."*

Again, as an assessor in a less mature program, this would typically be sufficient to move on with determining that the vendor has a solid handle on the AI risk associated with its use and their products.

Another area to assess as part of the AI risk due diligence is the data protection controls. Investigating their privacy at this level would require a look at their Data Privacy Framework Certification, as well as their Privacy page on the Trust Center to determine if there is enough information to give your program the level of data needed to assess and identify associated with this domain.

If your program is slightly more engaged, then the best practice for this vendor (based on the level of risk they pose to your organization) would be to examine their AI and Privacy-related policy and program documentation to determine maturity level and coverage. Again, this vendor is higher risk given the data they will have access to, their network connectivity, how the software will be used at your company, and use of AI. Given this information, it would warrant a closer look at the risks and getting a more transparent picture of your vendor's AI risk.

More Mature Programs

Programs that have advanced along the TPRM maturity ladder are likely to have a seasoned intake process that automatically triggers the IRA and all other subsequent due diligence and care activities. The introduction of this new risk (AI) presents a good opportunity to review your IRA to ensure it aligns with best practices. An inherent risk assessment is simply a set of triggers for other risk areas that need to be addressed after the IRA is completed. It also assists with tiering your vendor and determining it's criticality to your organization. Therefore, the number of questions should be roughly the same as the number of risk domains you cover within your organization. For example, if you have typical risk domains (cyber, privacy, legal, compliance, operational, financial, credit, BR/DR), then the IRA should only include questions related to triggers or risks that identify assessments for those domains. If your IRA contains 30 or more questions, it would be wise to review it for relevance in addition to adding the AI question "Does this vendor use or sell an AI-enabled product?"

Less Mature Programs

Ensure the program has the above clauses included in any AI product contract and look to track the version of the addendum or Master Service Agreement, as well as its renewal date. Tracking the version number can assist as updates are required to any agreements upon renewal.

Use-Case Contract

The contract with the vendor for an AI-enabled product will also require clause enhancements to ensure it lowers the risk to both organizations. Given this is an HR product with highly sensitive data, it is important to ensure the contractual obligations are clear to the vendor. All need to ensure the contract includes the following (as discussed in previous sections):

Right to Perform a Security Assessment

This is different than what is typically in most contracts, "right to audit." First, the right to audit is mostly aimed at financial auditors, not security or risk assessors. Secondly, the word "audit" immediately sets most people on the defensive. Thirdly, what your team will want the right to be able to do, on an ongoing basis and not once per year, is a "security assessment" and not an audit. Lastly, ensure the language around this allows you to receive timely information from the vendor in the event of an incident or breach.

Transparency and Accountability

Make sure the contract includes language requiring the vendor to maintain audit trails and provide transparency mechanisms that show how the AI operates and makes decisions. Also, ensure the AI's limitations are transparent and have mechanisms in place to address accountability if the model isn't working as expected.

Security and Liability

The contract should include measures that ensures the vendor can protect the AI and other data from cyberattacks and unauthorized access. It's important to consider potential risks and clearly define liability for biases, errors, or negative outcomes that may arise from the AI. Additionally, the contract should have provisions for risk management frameworks and plans to effectively handle any AI-related risk issues.

AI Role and Scope

It's important that any agreement clearly outlines how the AI system should be used, including detailed statements about what it is restricted from doing or performing. Make sure to clearly distinguish the responsibilities between the AI system and the human personnel involved in the process.

Data Use and Privacy

Contracts should include clear clauses on how sensitive data is handled for AI training, modifications, or other purposes. It's important to set guidelines for data retention and deletion to make sure data is stored securely and deleted when no longer needed. Additionally, confidentiality agreements should be in place to ensure that sensitive information is well-protected from any unauthorized access or use by AI.

Intellectual Property

Make sure to clearly specify who owns the AI system, the data used for training, and any content or work produced by the AI. Also, clarify who owns the input prompts given to the AI and anything it creates.

Other Clauses to Consider

Other key areas to consider include performance and service levels, as well as setting clear goals and metrics for the AI system. The agreement should also include language on compliance requirements, such as following current and future AI laws and standards. Additionally, there should be a clause for incident notification in case of any incident or breach. The agreement should also cover change controls with a clear process for managing and testing changes to the AI system. Finally, a force majeure clause is necessary to protect parties from liability due to unforeseen events that disrupt business operations.

More Mature Programs

Ensure any Cybersecurity or AI Addendum created by your organization is used for this vendor and that the terms are the most stringent due to the high-risk level.

Use-Case Continuous Monitoring

The maturity here becomes more pronounced as less mature programs tend to perform limited continuous monitoring activities.

Less Mature Programs

Less mature programs should focus almost exclusively on high-risk vendors. Since this vendor is High Risk, your organization would input this vendor into your vendor risk and reputation software. We will use a fake risk and reputation software called VendorView for the purposes of this use case. This software is like typical market solutions in this area; it scans the perimeter of vendor networks and looks for public-facing vulnerabilities. It also uses sinkholes and other intelligence to provide an external view of each vendor's relative risk. This stage of program maturity usually involves risk assessors monitoring for any alerts or alarms related to the vendor and acting on them if they meet their defined risk threshold.

More Mature Programs

This level of maturity would require a program to input OpusNox into VendorView for ongoing monitoring, as well as to leverage threat intelligence tools to provide additional data on the vendor This would enable correlation with multiple data sources to identify potential risks or threats with this vendor quickly and with more assurance it isn't a false positive.

Use-Case Disengagement

Let's now pretend that it has been a few years and our company has decided to part ways with OpusNox. How would each program maturity level deal with this process:

Less Mature Programs

Look into the system of record, whether that's a spreadsheet or a fancy relationship manager software, and make a checklist of the things this vendor has (as determined during onboarding) that need to be returned or turned off.

First, revoke all access, which is best achieved by automating the process to deactivate all user accounts and revoke access to systems, databases, and networks to prevent unauthorized entry. Depending on how the contracts are written, identify who owns the data and ensure it is either destroyed properly (with a Certificate of Destruction) or secured during any legal or regulatory hold. Deprovisioning of the AI application or system should be completed across all platforms (test, dev, production) and documented.

More Mature Programs

Programs that are more seasoned and practiced can do the same as noted above but should add a monitoring phase post offboarding. There is a monitoring period once a vendor is offboarded to ensure nothing lingers. Leverage your network and access monitoring teams at your organization to scan and alert your team if any instance of that vendor appears post disengagement. Run that scan for at least a month or a quarter to ensure there are no unknown connections or access from the vendor into the system of record.

Conclusion of Use-Case

While this is a not a real company, the assessment here is illustrative and intended to show how a less mature and more mature TPRM program should assess, monitor, and mitigate the risk associated with an AI-enabled vendor. Leverage this use case as a guide on steps your teams could take to integrate AI risk identification, assessment, and management process into your TPRM program.

CHAPTER 3

AI: Now and Future in TPRM

We've discussed many of the risks that come from AI and how to manage them in your own TPRM program and processes. There are several advantages and improvements to a TPRM program that result from Artificial Intelligence. Some of the advantages are tied to capabilities within specific software products as solutions, which we will share below. We will avoid using vendor names but instead use a description of the product or functionality.

Embrace Continuous Monitoring: AI Is the Death of PIT Assessments

Point-in-Time (PIT) assessments are what most organizations perform on their third parties. Inherent risk assessment, remote questionnaires, physical validation, yearly audits, SOC audits, and other types of assessments are all conducted at a specific moment in time and place. These assessment types will remain relevant and important for several more years, but it is likely that evidence-specific reviews (like the ones produced by AI products in this space) will be the assessment types that live on as an acceptable practice.

G. C. Rasner, M. C. Rasner, *AI and Third-Party Risk*,
https://doi.org/10.1007/979-8-8688-2465-4_3

There are two types of TPRM software vendors currently in this space, as seen by the authors. Those who are the longstanding players selling this software and are now adopting AI into their platforms. Then there are newer entrants where AI has been part of their core functionality since the beginning. These newer companies are exciting to watch as they approach TPRM and risk management from very unique perspectives. Some great solutions are already available, and more are on the horizon that will enable an organization to replace PIT assessments and see in near-real time how their vendors' security landscape is evolving, allowing for more proactive rather than reactive risk mitigation with third parties.

AI to Lower Resource Requirements

AI is already making a significant impact in reducing resource constraints, with many software products now able to review and process large volumes of documents and artifacts, essentially replacing analysts. Most TPRM programs are overwhelmed with data, as we often request multiple documents, artifacts, and follow-up documentation from vendors. However, a lot of this data and documentation is in formats that are difficult to analyze and assess quickly by humans. This creates a double problem: not only do we have to deal with a large amount of data but we also have to spend time translating it into our risk framework. This task is challenging for humans, as our eyes and minds can get tired, leading to errors in translation and judgment. It also takes a long time to read and process all this information.

AI-enabled TPRM products can now perform tasks that took humans hours to complete in minutes. There are TPRM and C-SCRM software packages that include this functionality, as well as other products outside this space that offer similar capabilities. The benefit of using TPRM software with AI to analyze artifacts for security data is the seamless integration. However, the downside is that it can lock you into a specific vendor product. If the product aligns well with your strategic goals, that's acceptable. When it no longer meets those goals, be honest and search for a better-fitting vendor.

Figure 3-1. *AI Can Help TPRM Programs*

AI to Lower Cycle Times

Similar to the above, there are software solutions inside and outside of the TPRM space that can use agents to process data and trigger workflows to reduce the time it takes for a process to complete. This software will significantly aid in automating repetitive tasks and help ensure the next steps are not missed. The AI software can make more "intelligent" decisions based on vendor type, risk level, and threat. There will still be a human in the loop needed, but this kind of solution will reduce operational overhead and accelerate the time to resolution.

AI to Replace Resource Needs

Of course, these initial AI-powered solutions will definitely shake things up, especially when it comes to managing third-party risk and supply chains. While this change promises to make our work more efficient and focused on risks in the long run, it might also bring some short-term challenges - like having fewer team members. As AI takes over those repetitive, dull tasks usually handled by junior team members, the need for analysts and assessors may naturally decrease, but this shift can ultimately lead to a more streamlined and risk-focused team.

AI will also add some resource needs, mainly with regards to AI-experts and subject-matter experts to train and manage AI. More about that in the next section.

Resources and AI – A Challenge

As AI becomes increasingly used by enterprises and small businesses, a disruptor in resources will emerge. Many jobs that are repetitive and can be performed by an AI agent or that process large amounts of data are likely to be eliminated or significantly reduced. Work roles will also change, as human oversight of AI will become a major part of many professionals' responsibilities: ensuring AI performs as expected and does not pose dangers or undue risks. We will discuss some of the most obvious challenges for the third-party risk management space, how it could potentially be impacted, and ways to potentially future-proof your program in later sections.

Entry-Level Conundrum

As we've talked about, it's quite likely that AI will begin taking on many of the repetitive and large-scale data review tasks that are currently handled by most TPRM programs. Tasks like reviewing SOC2 reports or policy documents in bulk to spot risks and then summarizing those findings into clear reports are areas where a well-trained AI can really shine. In a big company, these tasks are often managed by just a few people or even a whole team of four or more. Now, this workload can be reduced to just one person who reviews the AI's work and focuses on the more engaging and impactful parts assessing the risks, figuring out how to manage them, and applying higher-level thinking.

This and other tasks that would normally be performed by an entry-level teammate create a challenge for the program's growth. Reducing the number of people handling the work limits a company's options for future leaders. Additionally, reviewing all those documents was excellent training for new employees, but now the AI is doing the reviewing. That training and hands-on experience of recognizing a good SOC2 or policy document versus a poor one are somewhat lost with this work transfer.

There is no simple solution here because the loss of personnel is probably unavoidable, as that was the main reason for adopting the AI platform: to save costs for the company. However, if you have one or two people who would normally do entry-level work, do not let them rely too heavily on the AI. First, train them on how an assessor should review and evaluate all typical documentation (SOC2, policy documents, pentest results, etc.) so they can correctly determine if the AI is performing adequately. Second, they should conduct routine audits of the AI output to identify any issues. During these audits, they must compare the actual artifacts with the output to spot discrepancies. These two steps will help teach your team some critical basics as they do their work and could potentially lead the team forward.

Future-Proof Your Career and Program

Never stop learning, as it's such valuable advice from our mentors and leaders over the years. With AI, there are three exciting opportunities: first, for those who are experts in Artificial Intelligence; second, for those skilled in managing AI systems; and third, for specialists in other fields or subjects. If you have a strong math background, your expertise in AI can open doors to fantastic salary offers and signing bonuses. Keep exploring and growing - it's a rewarding journey!

Remember at the very beginning of this book we quoted the CEO of Walmart, the biggest employer in the United States, as saying

> *"It's very clear that AI is going to change literally every job," Chief Executive Doug McMillon said this week in one of the most pointed assessments to date from a big-company CEO on AI's likely impact on employment. Walmart executives aren't sugarcoating the message: Artificial intelligence will wipe out jobs and reshape its workforce. Some jobs and tasks at the retail juggernaut will be eliminated, while others will be created, McMillon said this week at Walmart's Bentonville headquarters during a workforce conference with executives from other companies. "Maybe there's a job in the world that AI won't change, but I haven't thought of it."*[1]

For those of us with average math skills, exploring options like becoming an AI operator or specializing in our chosen field can be really exciting. This is the perfect time to embrace the "don't stop learning" spirit in your career journey. If you're interested in learning how to navigate and be a part of AI systems, you might want to start with some of the many free or affordable online courses available. Platforms like Coursera, edX, Google AI Essentials, Kaggle Learn, and university programs such as the

[1] https://www.wsj.com/tech/ai/walmart-ceo-doug-mcmillon-ai-job-losses-dbaca3aa?mod=hp_lead_pos1

University of Helsinki's Elements of AI offer a wide range of resources suited for everyone - from beginners, like Andrew Ng's "AI for Everyone," to more technical and advanced courses like Harvard's CS50 Introduction to AI with Python. The good news is that many of these platforms allow you to audit courses at no cost, giving you full access to the materials without needing to pay for a certificate.

To train for AI as a beginner, focus on Google AI Essentials for a hands-on overview of AI fundamentals and prompting, IBM's AI for Everyone on Coursera for a non-technical introduction, or Andrew Ng's Machine Learning Specialization for a comprehensive, Python-based technical deep dive. Consider your goals: for practical application, choose the Google course; for a broad conceptual understanding, IBM's course; and for a strong technical foundation with coding, Andrew Ng's course is recommended.

Top institutions like Stanford Online, Microsoft, LinkedIn Learning, Harvard University, and Udemy offer AI courses for leaders. These programs aim to give executives the strategic know-how to integrate and lead AI initiatives in their organizations. The focus is on creating a strategic AI vision, building a culture that's ready for AI, ensuring AI is used ethically and responsibly, and using AI to gain a competitive edge - rather than just teaching technical programming skills.

Build a learning plan that serves as a roadmap aligned with your career goals, whether that is to become an AI engineer or an AI specialist. Key elements to include in your AI training are the basics, such as what AI, machine learning, and LLMs are, to understand the foundational core concepts. Learn to prompt effectively by mastering how to write clear and specific prompts, which is crucial for interacting with and maximizing AI tools. Practice with real-world scenarios using hands-on activities and examples to reinforce your understanding and apply your skills. Also, learn the fundamentals of generative AI and how it's used in practice, as this represents the next wave for AI.

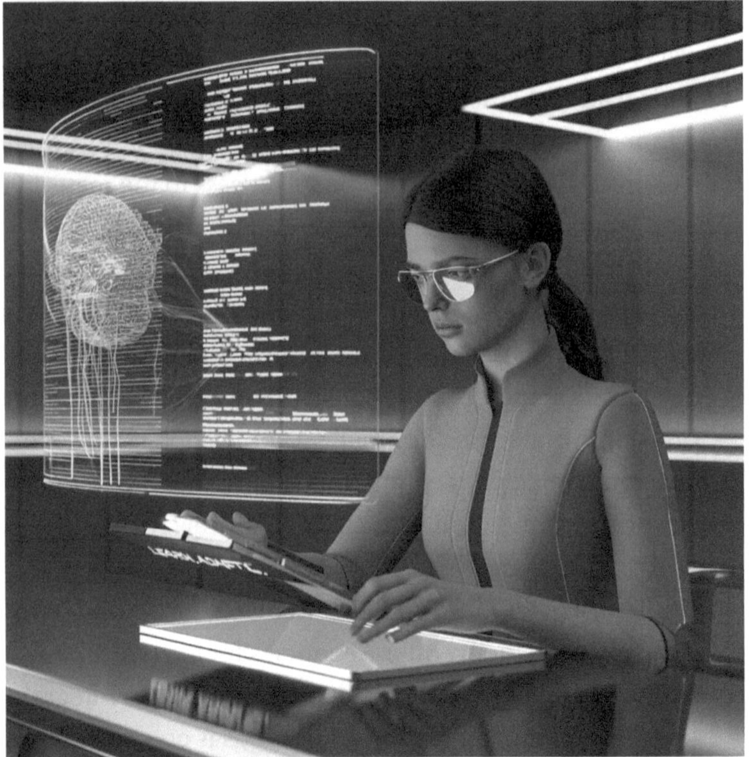

Figure 3-2. *Learn and Incorporate AI in Your Career Path*

The last group of people who can succeed in an AI economy are those who are experts in their field or domain. These individuals are in demand to help train AI agents and systems, oversee their work, audit them, and identify issues when an AI system does not produce the intended results. If you are early in your career and want to become a subject matter expert (SME) in your chosen field (other than AI), then you should certainly "never stop learning" to enhance your expertise and credentials. This involves obtaining appropriate and challenging certifications, teaching classes, taking courses, and contributing to your profession's knowledge base with articles, publications, and speeches.

If you're later in your career, make sure you've done everything mentioned above (hopefully) so you can confidently claim that expertise. Many people in this stage might face "imposter syndrome," where they feel inadequate for the "expert" title because they're aware of how much they still don't know, or they just feel unsure and lack confidence. Overcoming this takes regular practice with your subject, training yourself not to be too negative about your abilities. Challenge yourself to try new activities that boost your skills and help you present yourself better. For example, if you haven't done much public speaking in your field, find opportunities to practice because it will also help you become more confident in how you present yourself.

Going back to the statements and actions from Walmart, there is a great example of how the company is adapting and suggests how roles and opportunities will change with AI:

> *"Some changes are already rippling across the workforce. In recent years, Walmart has automated many of its warehouses with the help of AI-related technology, triggering some job cuts, executives said. Walmart is also looking to automate some back-of-store tasks.*
>
> *New roles have been established, too. Walmart, for example, created an "agent builder" position last month an employee who builds AI tools to help merchants. It expects to add people in areas like home delivery or in high-touch customer positions, such as its bakeries. The company has also added more in-store maintenance technicians and truck drivers in recent years."*[2]

[2]https://www.wsj.com/tech/ai/walmart-ceo-doug-mcmillon-ai-job-losses-dbaca3aa?mod=hp_lead_pos1

There will be new roles created (agent builders), old ones destroyed (back-of-store tasks), and some existing roles (truck drivers) expanded. Look for the new roles or existing role expansions for your future opportunities.

> *"AI is just starting to ripple through the job market," said Ronnie Chatterji, OpenAI's chief economist, at the Bentonville conference. "I think 18 to 36 months, you're going to see a lot more impact." Earlier this month, OpenAI unveiled a partnership with Walmart and other companies to design an AI-training certificate program.*
>
> *The drumbeat of warnings about AI-related job cuts has increased in recent months. Accenture CEO Julie Sweet told investors Thursday that the firm is "exiting" employees who can't be retrained for the AI age. Meanwhile, it will continue to hire people who are generative AI-fluent and retrain existing workers to serve clients in consulting and other divisions.... "I'm telling them, 'Guys, you are going to stay here, but you need to be the change agent. You need to evolve yourself,... "You're smart enough to work here, but you're not going to do the same job in two years. Embrace the moment."*[3]

Training and Certifications in AI

There are a number of paths and opportunities for those wanting to adopt more AI into their knowledge base. For those in the beginning of their AI journey, there are some good online courses that are free or near-free. Coursera[4] has a number of free courses on AI or courses that allow the introductory part of the longer offering to be taken without charge. Also

[3] https://www.wsj.com/tech/ai/walmart-ceo-doug-mcmillon-ai-job-losses-dbaca3aa?mod=hp_lead_pos1

[4] https://www.coursera.org/courses?query=artificial%20intelligence

offering free courses is Google's AI Essentials,[5] where you can build your AI skills with programs, training, and tools for most scenarios or use cases. The Introduction to Generative AI course is free and provides a badge. On Codecademy, there are some free courses that allow for hands-on work, such as "Prompt Engineering: Ethical Hacking & Generative AI Fusion" and "Intro to Large Language Models (LLMs)." All of these platforms offer a way to start for free and then advance in your knowledge with career path courses, skill path courses, or courses to learn a specific AI topic. The more advanced courses are not free, but depending on your situation, the investment in these courses is a good idea to continue your knowledge growth.

For beginner courses to get a foundation of AI, look to "AI for Everyone" from Coursera from Andrew Ng, who does a great job explaining this topic to any level of user.[6] Google AI's course "AI Essentials" gives the student a short course on AI foundations, prompt engineering, responsible use, and application of AI in daily use.[7] Internationally, the University of Helsinki provides a "Elements of AI" course that is comprehensive for an introduction with useful concepts.[8] Those are three choices that are free (currently) and can get anyone without technical skills into the AI universe easily.

For the next step, look to get some hands-on practice and projects to cement your AI learning into skills that can be leveraged at work. Google Machine Learning Crash Course is an excellent starting point for learning AI basics with hands-on exercises on foundational ML concepts.[9] Google AI also offers a similar experience to the ML offering and should

[5] https://ai.google/learn-ai-skills/

[6] https://www.coursera.org/learn/ai-for-everyone

[7] https://ai.google/learn-ai-skills/#:~:text=Learn%20AI%20basics,Learn%20More

[8] https://www.elementsofai.com

[9] https://developers.google.com/machine-learning/crash-course

be leveraged as well. Codecademy has interactive learning experiences and projects to assist learning in a more hands-on experience.[10] For those in AWS, there is a no-code platform, PartyRock, that allows for building generative AI applications to learn concepts such as prompt engineering.[11]

If your mode of learning is more structured, with a clear outcome or goal with steps, then the top three choices would be Coursera, Codecademy, and LinkedIn Learning. Coursera has a wide range of courses from a wide range of organizations (IBM AI Foundations, AI for Business, Google, Politecnico di Milano, and more), so it does not disappoint in the range of offerings. Codecademy has a lot of beginner-friendly offerings on specific AI skills with hands-on projects, such as building applications with AI. Almost everyone in professional life uses LinkedIn for networking, and LinkedIn Learning has been a good addition for professional development in recent years. Their courses offer certificate-level courses on generative AI and some practical skills in AI development and foundations.

Some of the key areas of focus on your AI learning path are to start with the fundamentals, which this book has started with the fundamentals learning. Machine Learning (ML) and Neural Networks (NN) are the next logical step to get the basics of AI models and how they learn from data. Learning about generative AI, its applications, and how it differs from ML and NN is important; then learn to write prompts with effective instructions so you can leverage AI tools. Add in some training on ethical use to understand the ethical implications and responsible AI use.

AI Certifications for Beginners

Certifications and certificates are important in your career path for a few reasons, but the authors' experience as both individual contributors and hiring managers is there are two excellent reasons. First, to learn. It isn't

[10] https://www.codecademy.com/catalog/subject/artificial-intelligence

[11] https://partyrock.aws

just about the award of the certification after the exam, but the journey to get there involves a lot of learning. Second, the certifications are often used as sorting tools in resumes and candidate selection. The certification or certificate won't get you the job, but it can be important to ensure you stand out among candidates.

Foundational certificates offered from "AI for Everyone," "Google AI Essentials," and "IBM Introduction to Artificial Intelligence" are great starting points in your journey.[12] Some budget-friendly options are Uxcel, which has options from a number of institutions around the world; SkillUp[13] by Simplilearn is a free, self-paced AI and ML certificate program, and it even uses tools such as Python and TensorFlow for those more adventurous. For those interested in a cloud AI route, look at Azure AI Fundamentals or AWS Certified AI Practitioner, which are both excellent starting points for learning cloud AI and ML fundamentals without a lot of technical experience required.

Take advantage of the current atmosphere where companies are offering free or near-free introductions into AI to get more entrants into their products. Not only is it essential to learn to enable you to leverage this new technology in your career but it is also to place this learning and these achievements on your resume to advance your career.

Regulatory Guidance for AI

Regulatory guidance for Artificial Intelligence (AI) varies around the world and across different sectors. The European Union's AI Act offers a risk-based approach to regulation, while in the United States, agencies like the FDA focus on medical devices and drugs, and organizations like FINRA

[12] https://uxcel.com/blog/top-free-ai-certifications

[13] https://www.simplilearn.com/ai-engineer-course

oversee financial services by applying current rules to AI.[14] Common themes include assessing risks, ensuring transparency, managing data responsibly, and overseeing the entire life cycle of AI systems.

EU-AI Act

The EU AI Act is a historic regulation that sets unified rules for artificial intelligence (AI) systems across the European Union.[15] Its goal is to ensure AI is safe, respects fundamental rights, and promotes trustworthy AI. It classifies AI into risk levels: unacceptable, high, limited, and minimal, with unacceptable AI being banned and high-risk AI subject to strict requirements. The Act also covers General-Purpose AI (GPAI) models and applies to companies and organizations that develop, use, distribute, or import AI into the EU market, with hefty fines for those who do not comply.

[14] "Generative AI Security: Theories and Practices," by Ken Huang et al., Springer, 2024, pp. 61-63.

[15] `https://artificialintelligenceact.eu`

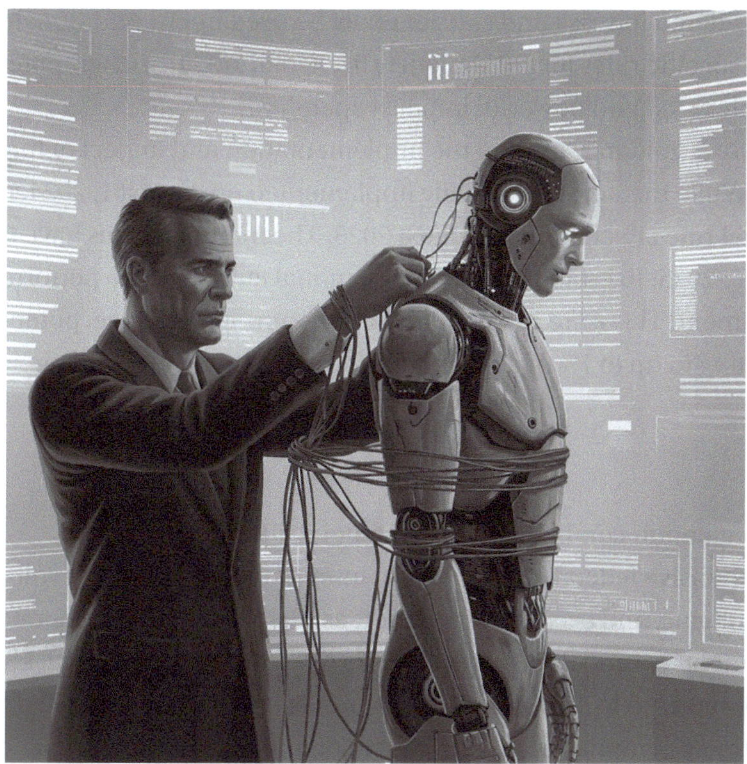

Figure 3-3. *EU Regulates AI*

The key points about the AI Act highlight its risk-based approach. It groups AI systems according to the level of potential harm they might cause to health, safety, and fundamental rights, ranging from minimal to unacceptable risk. For AI systems that present an unacceptable risk like government-run social scoring or those that manipulate human behavior there are outright bans. High-risk AI used in vital fields such as hiring, law enforcement, and employment must meet strict standards for data quality, human oversight, and transparency. AI systems with limited risk, like chatbots, are required to be transparent and must inform users that they are interacting with AI. Many everyday AI tools, such as spam filters, are considered low risk and can generally be used freely. Additionally, the Act has specific rules for GPAI models like OpenAI, due to their potential "systemic risks" and powerful impact capabilities.

There is guidance around the implementation and impact of the EU AI Act. While the Act was officially implemented on August 1, 2024, it has a gradual rule effect through August 2026. The member states have until August 2, 2025, to establish their own national authorities to perform enforcement. There are substantial fines for non-compliance, potentially amounting to up to 7% of a company's global annual gross income.

USA

US AI regulation combines state and federal efforts, lacking comprehensive federal legislation but integrating existing laws, voluntary commitments, and executive guidance, especially regarding federal government use and data privacy. While Congress is gradually tackling AI through targeted legislation and various bills have been introduced, the main strategy emphasizes agency enforcement, industry best practices, and state-level protections like Colorado's AI Act, which has set rules for high-risk AI systems.

The federal approach has been plagued by a lack of a single, overarching federal law that broadly regulates the development and use of AI. Much of the legislation has been done with AI-related provisions included in broader acts in the US Congress. Many have not been enacted as of this writing. In October 2023, the Biden administration issued an Executive Order on Safe, Secure, and Trustworthy Artificial Intelligence focusing on federal agency use, security, and critical infrastructure.

There are some US states that are striking out alone, the most notable being the Colorado AI Act, which mandates developers and deployers of high-risk AI systems to use reasonable care to prevent algorithms from discrimination and requires annual impact statements.

UK

The UK's approach to AI regulation is evolving from its earlier flexible, non-legislative principles to include potential laws, especially focusing on the most advanced AI models.[16] With the Labour Party now in power, attention is turning to creating a clear "statutory code" and specific safeguards for high-risk AI, such as setting up an "AI authority" to oversee regulation and handle copyright issues related to AI training data. While existing laws like GDPR still apply, the new government is eager to address regulatory gaps and promote responsible AI development by working together across sectors and establishing a centralized AI risk management framework. The UK's approach will continue to differ from the EU's more comprehensive and prescriptive AI Act, with the UK's regulations being more targeted and focused on specific high-risk systems.

The previous approach, which is Principles-Based, has the government initially focused on a "pro-innovation" approach using existing technology-neutral laws, avoiding dedicated AI legislation. The existing regulators, such as the Information Commissioner's Office (ICO), Ofcom, CMA, and the Financial Conduct Authority (FCA), were expected to apply AI principles within their sectoral contexts.

The upcoming approach, which the new Labour government is looking to deploy, is a "statutory code" and "targeted guardrails" for the most powerful AI models and general-purpose AI systems. Nothing specific has been recommended yet, but there are various proposals to establish a central AI authority to oversee the new regulatory approach and ensure a consistent approach. There is a plan to develop an AI risk register across the economy for the purpose of providing a central point of truth for all AI risks in the UK. Integral to this is copyright reform to address the concerns of creative artists and content creators.

[16] https://www.deloitte.com/uk/en/Industries/financial-services/blogs/the-uks-framework-for-ai-regulation.html

Singapore

Singapore adopts a flexible and voluntary approach to AI regulation, emphasizing model governance frameworks and industry-specific guidelines instead of comprehensive legislation.[17] Notable initiatives like the Model AI Governance Framework and its recent version for Generative AI offer helpful guidance to organizations on how to develop and use AI responsibly. Several government agencies, such as IMDA and PDPC, regularly provide guidelines to encourage responsible AI use across sectors like finance, healthcare, and data privacy. Overall, Singapore aims to support AI innovation while keeping safety, ethics, and public trust at the forefront.

The Model AI Governance Framework for 2019 and 2020 provided detailed and practical advice for the private sector on AI ethics and governance risks and issues. The Model AI Governance Framework for Generative AI in 2024 is an update that addresses specific challenges around generative AI challenges and risks.

[17] https://iapp.org/resources/article/global-ai-governance-singapore/#:~:text=Singapore%20has%20not%20enacted%20a,of%20the%20AI%20governance%20lifecycle.

Figure 3-4. *A Collaborative Approach with AI*

The key points of the framework are that it focuses on voluntary adoption of guidelines to enable AI to be adopted and expanded more quickly. It does take a risk-based approach and recommends focusing on higher-risk AI systems and services. It also ensures frameworks are built on principles of transparency, fairness, accountability, and humanity so it better aligns with international AI ethics.

There is some sector-specific guidance in this approach by Singapore:

- **Finance**: The Monetary Authority of Singapore (MAS) provides guidance, for example, the FEAT Principles, which are available for AI use in the financial services sector.

- **Healthcare**: The Ministry of Health (MOH) and the Health Sciences Authority (HAS) have guidelines for safe use of AI in healthcare services.
- **Privacy**: The Personal Data Protection Commission (PDPC) also has guidance on using personal data in an AI system.

South Korea

South Korea's AI Basic Act is a law that went into effect on January 22, 2026, after being signed on January 21, 2025.[18] It sets up a legal framework for developing and using AI. The Act tries to balance innovation with safety and ethics by putting regulations in place for "high-impact" AI systems, including risk assessments, transparency, and user notifications. Key parts of the Act include creating the National AI Committee to make policy and an AI Safety Institute to address risks, while also encouraging AI development, training for workers, and international cooperation.

The stated purpose of the South Korea Act is to protect human rights and dignity, improve the quality of life, and strengthen national AI competitiveness with sound development and trustworthy use of AI. The focus is primarily on high-impact AI systems, but it applies to the broader AI market and requires compliance from both foreign and domestic producers of AI products. For those high-risk AI systems, it mandates risk assessments, risk management plans, and transparency for all AI systems that could impact fundamental rights, safety, or human life.

There is a governance structure established with the National AI Committee, led by a president who oversees policy and a special AI Safety Institute to support the implementation of policy and identify and

[18] https://securiti.ai/south-korea-basic-act-on-development-of-ai/#:~:text=I.-,Introduction,effect%20from%20January%2024%2C%202026.

address potential AI risks. The Act requires companies to notify users when products or services use generative AI or high-impact AI systems to indicate when AI-generated content could cause confusion with "authentic" material.

There is an emphasis on promoting innovation, including measures to foster AI development with data utilization, support for AI startups in South Korea, professional workforce development to upscale existing resources for an AI economy, and helping to build out the necessary infrastructure to support AI.

Enforcement is primarily through the Ministry of Science and ICT (MSIT) as the regulatory body to investigate any suspected violations and issue orders to correct or cease-and-desist, if required. There is a one-year transition period before full enforcement to allow businesses to adapt and get their AI systems and governance up to meet the new Act's requirements.

United Arab Emirates

The UAE oversees AI with a thorough framework that includes the National Strategy for AI 2031, gentle AI Ethics Principles, and existing data protection laws like the Personal Data Protection Law (PDPL).[19] They are also leading the way in AI governance by harnessing AI itself to help craft and update laws through the Regulatory Intelligence Office. This effort is all about making the legislative process smoother, faster, and more in tune with everyone's needs. The key principles guiding this work focus on being transparent, responsible, fair, and safe, with a special emphasis on ethical progress and strong governance for AI technologies.

[19] https://www.whitecase.com/insight-our-thinking/ai-watch-global-regulatory-tracker-uae

The focus from the UAE is to promote a national strategy for AI by 2031. Launched in 2017, this strategy aims to position the UAE as a global AI leader and includes a goal for strong governance and effective regulation. AI Ethics Principles and Guidelines were introduced in December 2022; these are non-binding guidelines promoting the ethical, fair, and responsible use of AI across sectors. The UAE is using AI to power a Regulatory Intelligence Office that analyzes data to identify, draft, and suggest updates to laws, making the legislative process more efficient.

Their approach is to leverage existing legal frameworks and AI systems are governed under existing technology-neutral laws such as the Personal Data Protection Law (PDPL), which requires compliance with principles of data protection, fairness, and accountability. The UAE AI framework in the UAE is built on seven principles:

1. **Transparency and Accountability**: AI systems need to be transparent and explainable, with their operators documenting their use and data flows.
2. **Fairness and Non-Discrimination**: AI should prioritize fairness and avoid bias or discrimination.
3. **Robustness and Safety**: Systems must be reliable and prioritize both physical and digital safety.
4. **Human-Centered Values**: AI development should respect fundamental human values and rights.
5. **Strategic Approach**: The UAE takes a proactive and forward-thinking approach:
6. **Leading with AI**: Instead of just regulating AI, the UAE is using AI to actively participate in its own governance, serving as a testbed for AI-driven legislative processes.

7. **Integrated Framework**: The regulation combines strategic national goals with practical ethical guidelines and the application of existing laws, especially data protection laws.

Japan

Japan has introduced the AI Promotion Act, a welcoming step toward encouraging AI development and deployment.[20] Since taking effect in June 2025, this law emphasizes cooperation and responsible AI use, aligning with national goals, promoting transparency, and fostering international partnerships. It builds on existing laws, encourages voluntary guidelines for businesses, and is overseen by a high-level AI strategy headquarters. The approach avoids rigid rules, focusing instead on nurturing responsible AI innovation and growth.

The focus of their regulation is on innovation by aiming to prioritize the promotion of AI research, development, and use. The approach is viewed as a light touch with a framework that favors cooperation and voluntary compliance rather than a strict set of rules and penalties. The UAE has established dedicated bodies like the UAE Council for Artificial Intelligence and Blockchain to oversee AI integration and regulatory approaches to focus on governance.

China

China has enacted comprehensive AI regulations, focusing on algorithm recommendation, deep synthesis, and generative AI, with key measures including the Administrative Provisions on Recommendation Algorithms (2022), the Deep Synthesis Provisions (2023), and the Provisional Provisions on Generative AI Services (2023), supplemented by the

[20] https://www.diligent.com/resources/blog/japan-ai-regulations

upcoming Measures for Labeling Artificial Intelligence-Generated Content (effective September 1, 2025).[21] These regulations require mandatory labeling of synthetic content, real-name registration for users of deep synthesis services, and algorithm filings to the Cyberspace Administration of China (CAC) for services influencing public opinion. China's approach also includes national standards and local initiatives to foster AI development while balancing security and public safety.

There are some key regulations around the way China is managing its AI risk and industry.

- **Administrative Provisions on Recommendation Algorithms (2022)**: The regulation oversees recommendation algorithms, asking providers to submit their algorithms to the CAC and set up ways for users to opt out of personalized suggestions, making the process more transparent and user-friendly.
- **Administrative Provisions on Deep Synthesis (2023)**: This regulation covers deepfakes and other synthetic media, encouraging users to register with their real names, seek consent before editing personal details, and clearly label AI-generated content. It aims to promote transparency and protect user rights, making online interactions safer and more trustworthy content.
- **Provisional Provisions on Generative AI Services (2023)**: Sets clear guidelines for managing generative AI services, emphasizing safety, data privacy, and ethical practices in their development and use.

[21] https://www.whitecase.com/insight-our-thinking/ai-watch-global-regulatory-tracker-china

- **Measures for Labeling Artificial Intelligence-Generated Content (2025)**: Starts implementing mandatory labels for AI-generated content in September 2025, expanding on existing rules for deepfake and generative AI technologies.
- **Data-Related Laws**: Laws like the Cybersecurity Law, Personal Information Protection Law (PIPL), and Data Security Law also govern data privacy and security aspects of AI.

The key principles behind their approach can be viewed as a few key goals:

- **National Approach:** Various national and industry standards have been put in place to support these regulations, covering essential security needs for generative AI and labeling methods for AI-generated content.
- **Pro-Innovation/Growth Stance:** As China implements these regulations, it also warmly signals its support for growth in the industry, aiming to bring stakeholders together and speed up technological advancements.
- **Mandatory Labeling:** AI-generated content, especially deepfakes, must be clearly labeled to prevent public confusion.
- **Real-Name Registration:** Users of deep synthesis services are required to register with their real names.
- **Algorithm Filings:** Providers of online information services that can influence public opinion must file their algorithms with the CAC.

- **Emphasis on Safety and Ethics:** China's regulations emphasize safety, control, and ethical standards, creating a responsible environment. However, they also bring up worries about censorship and limitations on free expression, which many find challenging to free speech rights.

China is a big player in the AI field and, as such, has positioned its regulatory framework to deal with the risk while attempting to thread the needle of pro-growth.

India

India is taking thoughtful steps toward AI regulation. While it doesn't yet have full AI-specific laws, the country is working on a balanced approach that combines existing data protection laws with new guidelines from the Ministry of Electronics and Information Technology (MeitY).[22] These guidelines emphasize the importance of immediate due diligence, responsible AI development, and requiring government approval before deploying certain AI models. Additionally, India's National Strategy for Artificial Intelligence (2018) encourages responsible AI use, and the recent Digital Personal Data Protection Act, 2023, helps govern data processing related to AI. The government aims for a "light-touch" regulatory style that encourages innovation while ensuring safety, supporting the growth of a strong, national AI ecosystem.

Several existing laws are in place to address AI risks and frameworks. For instance, the Information Technology Act, 2000 (IT Act), along with the Information Technology (Intermediary Guidelines and Digital Media

[22] https://iapp.org/resources/article/global-ai-governance-india/#:~:text=India's%20AI%20policy%20has%20two,purview%20of%20its%20legislative%20scope's%20AI%20policy%20has%20two,purview%20of%20its%20legislative%20scope

Ethics Code) Rules, 2021, and the Digital Personal Data Protection Act, 2023, help regulate important aspects like data privacy and the prevention of deepfakes. Additionally, the MeitY Advisory issued in March 2024 provides guidance for AI platforms and intermediaries. It encourages them to follow due diligence, work to prevent algorithmic bias, and seek government approval before deploying certain unproven AI models.

International Initiatives and Cooperation

There are several international bodies that are striving to get a more uniform, international approach to AI guidelines and conduct. There is a general agreement that an international-based approach is ideal, but it is unlikely to happen due to conflicts between nation-states on goals and strategies for AI and their own futures.[23]

G7

The G7 has launched the "Hiroshima AI process" to encourage international efforts in creating voluntary AI guidelines and practices.[24] The Hiroshima AI Process (HAIP) serves as a comprehensive policy framework set during Japan's G7 Presidency in 2023, emphasizing responsible AI governance. It is built on four key pillars: examining AI risks and potential benefits, establishing International Guiding Principles, developing a voluntary Code of Conduct for advanced AI developers, and fostering project-based collaborations on responsible AI tools. This initiative reached a milestone with the introduction of the HAIP Reporting

---

[23] "Generative AI Security: Theories and Practices," by Ken Huang et al., Springer, 2024, pp. 89–92

[24] `https://www.ey.com/en_gl/insights/ai/g7-ai-principles-and-code-of-conduct#:~:text=The%20G7%20AI%20Principles,key%20aspects%20of%20AI%20governance.`

Framework in February 2025, hosted by the OECD, which helps oversee the adoption of the Code of Conduct and promotes greater transparency and accountability in AI development worldwide.

***Figure 3-5.** Focus on Sustainability and Responsible AI*

OECD

The OECD has developed a set of AI principles.[25] The OECD AI Principles offer a worldwide guide based on five core values for responsible and trustworthy AI. Since their adoption in 2019 and update in 2024, they've

25 https://oecd.ai/en/ai-principles

been a helpful resource for AI developers and policymakers. These principles encourage creating AI that is innovative and beneficial while also respecting human rights, democratic values, and promoting sustainable development. The key principles include fostering inclusive growth, supporting sustainable development and well-being, prioritizing human-centered values and fairness, ensuring transparency and explainability, and emphasizing robustness, security, and safety Accountability.

The five principles are supported by several goals and controls.

1. Inclusive Growth, Sustainable Development, and Well-Being.
    a. Promote AI for the benefit of people and the planet.
    b. Aim to reduce inequalities and protect natural environments.
    c. Support the development of AI systems that enhance human capabilities.
2. Human-Centered Values and Fairness
    a. Ensure AI systems are designed to respect the rule of law, human rights, and democratic values.
    b. Include mechanisms to guarantee non-discrimination, equality, dignity, and fairness for individuals.
    c. Address potential societal harm and protect freedoms, like freedom of expression, while mitigating risks from misinformation.
3. Transparency and Explainability
    a. Encourage mechanisms that make AI systems understandable.
    b. Promote clarity on data sources, processes, and decision-making within the AI system life cycle.

4. Robustness, Security, and Safety
   a. Mandate that AI systems are secure, safe, and function appropriately throughout their life cycle.
   b. Require that AI systems can be safely overridden, repaired, or decommissioned if they pose risks of undue harm.
5. Accountability
   a. Establish that AI actors are responsible for the proper functioning of AI systems and adherence to the principles.
   b. Require risk management approaches and traceability to enable analysis of system performance and responses to inquiries.

UN

The United Nations established an AI Advisory Body in 2024.[26] The United Nations AI Advisory Body is a diverse group of 39 experts from government, civil society, academia, and the private sector. They were created to guide the international management of artificial intelligence and are working toward a final report, Governing AI for Humanity, due in September 2024. Co-chaired by Carme Artigas and James Manyika, this body is part of the UN Secretary-General's efforts to make sure AI benefits everyone in our global community. The body contained members from a diverse set of backgrounds, regions, and expertise, and included representatives from large AI and technology companies such as Sony, OpenAI, and Microsoft.

[26] https://news.un.org/en/story/2024/09/1154541#:~:text=Globally%20inclusive%20architecture,on%20international%20cooperation%20and%20transparency

The main purpose of the advisory board was to analyze the challenges and opportunities presented by AI, provide high-level recommendations for the international community on the governance of AI, ensure that AI's potential benefits are used for good, and address the need for an inclusive approach to AI governance, particularly in the Southern Hemisphere. The key outcomes of the advisory board's work were laid out in a final report[27] in September 2024. The report recommended the regular assessment of the state of AI, harmonizing standards, safety, and risk management for AI globally, and anchoring governance for AI within the UN Charter, human rights law, and the Sustainable Development Goals.

Conclusion

Artificial intelligence is now real. It can be a complex system and appear to be a "black box" to most of those without deep math and AI knowledge. One of our mentors once described it better as "enhanced intelligence" rather than artificial. Her point was that the term "Artificial Intelligence" has so much wrapped up in it that it is not actually real but science fiction and Hollywood. Thinking of it as Enhanced Intelligence makes it more accurate: this isn't an artificial brain making decisions, it is an enhanced decision-making machine that enhances intelligence, not replace it.

The risks of AI in our lives are already upon us in real-world issues and breaches. There are numerous examples in the last five years of AI bias, AI hallucinations, and AI-caused breaches to demonstrate that the threat is real. Many of the readers of this book are not surprised by this, but the real concern is if this is what happens with it being so new, imagine how bad it will be in five years?!

---

[27] https://www.un.org/sites/un2.un.org/files/governing_ai_for_humanity_final_report_en.pdf

Risk is the possibility of something bad happening. Third-party risk management is the program and process of identifying, assessing, and managing your vendor risk. There are excellent frameworks organizations can adopt for managing that risk, and there are also frameworks to manage cyber supply chain risk if that is your organization's focus.

There are a number of potential risks with AI. AI can be prone to hallucinations when it comes to conclusions that aren't supported by the facts. There is always the risk of a data leak given the vast amounts of data AI consumes. Many AI systems can lack transparency, making it hard to analyze how they work and their accuracy. There is the risk of someone manipulating the data or using AI to manipulate. One of the more concerning risks in AI is that of bias and having it unfairly favor one group over another without merit.

Assessing AI risk at a vendor can take a number of forms, but one of the keys to success is choosing a risk framework for AI. There are a number of choices, which we reviewed throughout this book. We spent a good deal of time on the NIST AI Risk Management Framework 1.0 due to its relative popularity and its ability to be translated into other frameworks and languages. The importance of a framework is two-fold: first, it ensures your program and processes are complete and not merely a "bucket of best practices"; second, as threats and risks change, which they always do, frameworks ensure you can update your program and processes accordingly.

Figure 3-6. *AI and TPRM Working Together*

Assessing AI risk within TPRM phases is designed to help organizations understand the scope of risk and impact in each of these phases. Governance and Oversight, Pre-Contract, Contract Review, Continuous Monitoring, Disengagement, and Continuous Improvement phases will all require some changes to your program and process to account for AI risk. We used the example of Workday, which has a case study on the NIST AI RMF website, to walk a team through each phase and how they identify, assess, and mitigate AI risks.

The bulk of the book is focused on these AI risks, but there are some upsides or benefits as well. For example, there is already TPRM software that leverages AI to process all your third-party artifacts to respond to a SIG assessment. AI also has the potential to improve analysis and efficiency in TPRM programs significantly. However, as those efficiency gains are absorbed, it is likely to see a dip in the number of employment opportunities in TPRM and other fields. Getting AI into your career path is the best option to increase your chances of remaining relevant.

The book finished up with an overview of global regulations, the strongest regulation being the EU AI Act. Many of the other nations on the list take a more hands-off, pro-innovation approach (Singapore, South Korea, Japan, UK) or have no central legislation to speak of (USA).

It has only been 11 years since the OCC first promulgated to big US financial institutions that they had to manage the risk of third parties (2014). In that time, there have been many changes and new risks added. Artificial intelligence is a new risk, but with the tools and best practices in this book, it can be managed as "just another risk."

Glossary of Terms

Advanced Persistent Threat (APT): A long-term, sophisticated cyberattack where an unauthorized user gains undetected access to a system or network.

Algorithm: A set of instructions or rules that a computer system follows to complete a task or solve a problem.

Anonymization: A process that alters personal data so that it can no longer be related to a specific individual, even by re-identification techniques.

Anti-Virus Software: A program that prevents, detects, and removes malware from computer systems.

Artificial General Intelligence (AGI): A hypothetical future AI that could understand, learn, and solve any problem a human can.

Artificial Intelligence (AI): The broad field of computer science focused on creating machines or software that can perform tasks typically requiring human intelligence, such as problem-solving, decision-making, and language understanding.

Artificial Narrow Intelligence (ANI): AI systems designed to perform a specific, narrow task, which is the current state of AI technology.

Attack Surface: The sum of the different points where an unauthorized user can try to enter or extract data from a system.

Authentication: The process of verifying the identity of a user or device to ensure they are who they claim to be.

Authorization: The process of verifying that a user or process has the necessary permissions to access a specific resource or perform a given action.

G. C. Rasner, M. C. Rasner, *AI and Third-Party Risk*,
https://doi.org/10.1007/979-8-8688-2465-4

Availability: The property of being accessible and usable on demand by authorized users.

Bias: Skewed or unfair patterns in AI model outputs that result from biased training data or assumptions made during learning.

Business Continuity Plan (BCP): A strategic plan outlining how an organization will continue operations during and after a significant disruption.

Chatbot: A software program designed to simulate conversation with human users through text or voice, often used for customer support or information retrieval.

Consent: A freely given, specific, and informed agreement from a data subject for their personal data to be processed.

Consequence: The actual damage or harm resulting from a risk event.

Controls: A process and/or activity used to monitor, review, or address a specific risk.

Cybersecurity Risk: The risk that a third party's unpatched systems or weak controls could be exploited, leading to a data breach affecting your organization's or your customers' data.

Data Breach: Any incident involving unauthorized or unlawful access, disclosure, or loss of personal data.

Data Controller: The entity that determines the purposes and means of processing personal data.

Data Lineage: Recording the origin, movement, and transformation of data over time.

Data Minimization: The principle that organizations should collect and retain only the minimum amount of personal data necessary for a specific purpose.

Data Processor: An individual or entity that processes personal data on behalf of a controller.

Data Subject Request (DSR): A request by an individual to exercise their rights regarding their personal data, such as access, rectification, or erasure.

Data Subject: An individual, directly or indirectly identifiable by the data collected about them.

DDoS Attack: A malicious attempt to disrupt the normal traffic of a targeted server, service, or network by overwhelming it with a flood of internet traffic.

Deep Learning: A type of machine learning that uses deep neural networks with multiple layers to understand complex patterns in large datasets.

Due Diligence: The process of thoroughly investigating and assessing a potential third party to understand their security, compliance, and operational posture.

Environmental, Social, and Governance (ESG) Risks: Risks associated with environmental damage, human rights issues, and governance failures within the supply chain.

Financial Risk: The potential for significant financial losses as a direct or indirect result of a third-party failure, breach, or operational disruption.

Firewall: A network security device that monitors and controls incoming and outgoing network traffic based on predetermined security rules.

Generative AI: A type of AI designed to generate new content, including text, images, music, or video, often by learning from existing data.

Geopolitical Risks: Risks stemming from political instability, trade wars, or changes in government regulations in different regions.

Impact: The magnitude of the negative effect or consequence of a risk event.

Inherent Risk: The level of risk before any control activities are evaluated.

Large Language Model (LLM): AI models trained on massive text datasets, enabling them to understand, generate, and manipulate human-like language.

Likelihood: The probability or frequency of a risk event occurring.

Machine Learning (ML): A subfield of AI that enables systems to learn from data without explicit programming, identifying patterns and making predictions or decisions.

Malware: Software designed to infiltrate or damage a computer system without the owner's consent.

Monitoring: The ongoing process of continuously assessing third-party performance, security, and compliance to ensure they continue to meet the organization's standards and expectations.

Multi-Factor Authentication (MFA): An extra layer of security that requires two or more different methods of verification to access an account, such as a password and a code from a mobile app.

Natural Language Processing (NLP): A branch of AI focused on enabling computers to understand, interpret, and generate human language.

Neural Network: A computational model inspired by the structure and function of the human brain, often used in deep learning for tasks like pattern recognition.

Onboarding: The process of formally bringing on a new third party, which includes initial assessment, contract finalization, and the establishment of security and oversight protocols.

Operational Risk: The risk of business disruptions, service outages, or supply chain issues at a vendor that negatively impact your organization's ability to operate.

Penetration Testing (Pen Testing): A simulated cyberattack on a system to evaluate its security by identifying vulnerabilities that a real attacker could exploit.

Personal Identifiable Information (PII): Any information that relates to an identifiable individual.

Phishing: An attempt to trick individuals into revealing sensitive information (like passwords or credit card details) by posing as a trustworthy entity.

Privacy by Design: An approach where privacy considerations are integrated into the design of systems and projects from the outset.

Prompt Engineering: The process of designing, refining, and optimizing prompts to elicit the desired and most effective responses from AI models.

Prompt: The input, instruction, or question given to an AI model, particularly an LLM, to generate a response.

Ransomware: Malware that encrypts a user's files and demands a ransom for their decryption.

Regulatory Risk: The risk of fines, penalties, or legal action due to a third party's failure to comply with relevant laws, regulations, and contractual obligations.

Reputational Risk: The potential for damage to an organization's brand and customer trust if a third-party incident, such as a breach or failure, occurs.

Residual Risk: The level of risk remaining after control activities have been evaluated.

Responsible AI: The ethical framework and practice of designing, developing, and deploying AI systems in a way that is safe, fair, and beneficial to society.

Risk Appetite: The amount and type of risk an organization is willing to takc on to achieve its objectives.

Risk Assessment: The process of identifying, analyzing, and evaluating risks to understand their potential impact and likelihood of occurring.

Risk Mitigation: Actions taken to reduce the likelihood or impact of a risk, or both.

Risk Owner: The individual or unit responsible for monitoring and managing a specific risk and its associated mitigation activities.

Risk Register: A formal document that lists identified risks, their potential impacts, and planned mitigation strategies.

Risk Response: A strategy for dealing with identified risks, which can include avoiding, accepting, reducing, or sharing the risk.

Risk: The possibility of an event occurring and its potential negative impact on objectives.

Supply Chain Resilience: The ability of a supply chain to effectively respond to and recover from disruptions.

Supply Chain Risk Management (SCRM): A systematic process of identifying, assessing, and mitigating potential risks within a supply chain to ensure continuity and resilience.

Supply Chain Risk Management: A broader concept encompassing risks within an organization's entire supply chain, including risks introduced by its own vendors and suppliers.

Supply Chain Risk: The potential for a supply chain to experience failures or disruptions that negatively impact operations, reputation, or financial stability.

Third Party: An external entity such as a vendor, supplier, partner, contractor, or service provider that interacts with your organization and has access to internal data, systems, or processes, regardless as to whether a contract is in place or monies are exchanged.

Third-Party Risk Management (TPRM): The structured process an organization uses to identify, assess, monitor, and mitigate the risks associated with its third-party relationships throughout their entire lifecycle.

Third-Party Risk: The potential for harm or negative impacts to an organization stemming from its relationship with a third party, including financial loss, data breaches, operational disruptions, or reputational damage.

Threat: A potential event or action that could cause harm to assets, operations, or people.

Tokenization: The process of breaking down text into smaller units, or tokens, for AI models to process and understand.

Transformer Model: A type of neural network architecture that has become fundamental to many LLMs, particularly effective for processing sequential data like language.

Trojan Horse: Malware disguised as legitimate software to trick users into installing it.

Uncertainty: A lack of knowledge or information about potential events or their outcomes.

Vendor Risk Management (VRM): Often used interchangeably with TPRM, this term specifically focuses on mitigating risks associated with vendors and service providers.

Virus: A type of malware that can replicate itself and spread to other systems.

Vulnerability: A weakness or flaw in a system, software, or process that can be exploited by an attacker to gain unauthorized access.

Index

A

B

C

G. C. Rasner, M. C. Rasner, *AI and Third-Party Risk*,
https://doi.org/10.1007/979-8-8688-2465-4

D

E

F

G

H

I, J, K

L

M

N

U

V

W, X, Y, Z